Global Expansion

Global Expansion

Britain and its Empire, 1870–1914

Willie Thompson

Pluto Press

LONDON • STERLING, VIRGINIA

First published 1999 by Pluto Press
345 Archway Road, London N6 5AA
and 22883 Quicksilver Drive, Sterling, VA 20166–2012, USA

British Library Cataloguing in Publication Data
A catalogue record for this book is available from the British Library

ISBN 0 7453 1240 3 hbk

Library of Congress Cataloging in Publication Data

Thompson, Willie.
    Global expansion : Britain and its empire, 1870–1914 / Willie Thompson.
        p.   cm. – (Pluto critical history)
    ISBN 0–7453–1240–3
    1. Great Britain—Colonies—History—19th century. 2. Great Britain—
    Colonies—History—20th century. I. Title. II. Series.
    DA16.T47 1999   99–35519
    941.081–dc21   CIP

Designed and produced for Pluto Press by
Chase Production Services, Chadlington, OX7 3LN
Typeset from disk by Composition & Design Services, Minsk, Belarus
Printed in the EC by T. J. International, Padstow

Contents

Chronology

1869 – Suez Canal opened.
1872 – Disraeli's Crystal Palace speech.
1872 – Sir Bartle Frere signs anti-slavery treaty with Sultan of Zansibar.
1875 – Disraeli purchases block of Suez Canal shares.
1877 – Unsuccessful British attempt to annex Boer republics.
1879 – Anglo-French control over Egyptian finances.
1879 – Zulu War.
1882 – Egypt invaded and taken under British control.
1884–85 – Berlin Congress establishes rules for African partition, hands over Congo basin to Leopold II.
1885 – General Gordon killed in Khartoum.
1886 – Upper Burma annexed.
1886 – Sir George Goldie receives Royal Charter, begins to extend control over Nigeria.
1886 – Transvaal goldfields opened.
1888 – Protectorates over northern Borneo.
1888 – William Mackinnon receives Royal Charter, unsuccessfully probes into Great Lakes region.
1889 – Cecil Rhodes receives Royal Charter, begins conquest of Matebeleland.
1889–90 – Anglo-French territorial agreements on West Africa.
1890 – Anglo-German territorial agreements on East Africa.
1891 – Nyasaland acquired as protectorate.
1895 – Uganda acquired as protectorate.
1895 – British overrun Ashanti and annex to Gold Coast.
1896 – Conquest of Sudan begins.
1896 – British-controlled Malaya organised as Federation of Malay States.
1897–9 – European scramble for concessions in China.
1898 – Territorial disputes with French on Niger.
1898 – Sudan conquered.
1898 – Fashoda Crisis – confrontation with French expedition on the Upper Nile.
1899 – Anglo-French territorial agreements on Sudan.
1899 – South African War (Boer War) begins.
1899 – Withdrawal of Royal Niger Company charter.
1900 – Australian colonies federated.
1900 – European states co-operate to suppress Chinese national rebellion (Boxer Rising).
1902 – South African War ends.
1907 – Anglo-Russian entente effectively partitions Persia.
1908 – Young Turk revolution.
1909 – Further British acquisitions in Malaya.
1910 – Union of South Africa.
1911 – Revolution in China.

Preface

This short volume focuses upon the British empire and the development and growth of the country's imperial system between 1870 and the outbreak of World War I, in the context of historically unprecedented global expansion by certain European powers. The British was incomparably the largest both in area and population of the European overseas empires of that period (and the land-based territorial expansions of the United States and the Russian empire). The historical meaning of what was taking place is of course only understandable in the context of the parallel activities of these other European powers – resulting from time to time in clashes and confrontations between rival empire-builders – and also, it must be stressed, in the historical novelty of the international imperial framework which emerged during those years. As is explained in the Introduction, the British empire, from its beginnings a commercial enterprise, had been central to the growth of Britain as an industrial power from the eighteenth to the middle of the nineteenth century, but from the 1870s it began to take on a new form and character.

In pursuing this theme an immediate problem of definition has to be noted. Britain's 'imperial system', amazingly complex though it was, is relatively straightforward to recognise, but 'imperialism', the word which was increasingly used to define the newly developing state of affairs, is a much vaguer and more nebulous concept – though no less of a reality. Clearly it has economic, political, cultural and military dimensions; it has implications in all of these for the imperial country no less than the subjected territories – and the latter may include formally independent states as well as those over which the imperial metropolis claims legal sovereignty.

At this point the difficulties are only beginning. The initial problem can be solved in a rough and ready manner on the analogy of the elephant – it may be hard or even impossible to propose a precise definition, but it is easy enough to recognise the creature when it actually presents itself. Much more problematic is to explain what was taking place. Did the 1870s really mark a significant break with what had gone before? If they did, what accounted for the expansion of European power by conquest or diplomacy over virtually every region of the globe? What were the meaning and consequences of the process for the populations which experienced the impact of this power? Was the escalation in international tensions which finally exploded in 1914 connected to such processes, either tightly or loosely? What if anything distinguished the expansion of British imperial power from that of France, Germany, Portugal, Italy or Belgium?

A prodigious quantity of research and writing has been devoted to trying to answer these and similar questions since the first general interpretations of imperialism began to appear in the early part of the twentieth century. Even the literature on particular aspects is vast. According to Andrew Porter, 'the secondary literature on the economics of empire-building is staggering in its extent, and is already the subject of valuable general surveys, both bibliographical and analytical'.[1] His short volume just quoted lists a bibliography of 321 items, most of them recent.

Historians learn to distrust apparent discontinuities in the historical record, and certainly strong continuities can always be found between different phases of historical development, but it is hard to avoid the conclusion that a marked change of tempo occurred during the last third of the nineteenth century in several dimensions of European reality – in the functioning of its economic systems, the nature of the relationship between its sovereign states, the internal character of and the interaction between its social classes, and the political and cultural outlook of its masses. The word 'imperialism' sums up the nature of that transformation. The economic framework of the change is sketched in Chapter 1, primarily so far as it concerned Britain.

For subsequent generations of historians and political analysts the debate around imperialism has been dominated, whether through repulsion or attraction, by Lenin's pamphlet of 1916, *Imperialism, the Highest Stage of Capitalism*. Much of that debate has been directed towards substantiating, modifying or refuting its theses. As several historians, both Marxist and non-Marxist, have pointed out,[2] Lenin wrote this massively researched pamphlet (the notes compiled in preparation run to over 700 printed pages) not to explain the history of colonial expansion but the reasons for the outbreak of general European war and the reasons why the proletariats of Europe mostly supported their governments in waging it. Nevertheless, it *does* assert a strong connection between the consolidation of monopoly capitalism, the export of capital and the seizure of colonies in the late nineteenth century. All of these things were certainly evident phenomena of the period: the question is whether they were causally related.

The lack of consensus on this argument persists, and this volume is not concerned to resolve it. Nevertheless, even in what is primarily a descriptive account of one particular imperialism, the issue unavoidably lurks in the background, and my own general standpoint will become clear in the course of the text. For the moment, however, personal observation may be in order.

Although this particular issue has not been central to my academic concerns, it is one in which I have continued to be interested since my undergraduate years. It intrigued me both because that time coincided with the early 1960s and the height of decolonisation struggles in Africa and because the imperialism of the 1870–1914 era appeared so significant for the subsequent history of the twentieth century. At that time I read Lenin's *Imperialism*, which did indeed seem to supply the key to understanding what had happened – but not for long. It became clear from the criticisms which were being directed at it at the time that – whatever the other merits of the pamphlet might be – as an explanation for what had happened in Africa and the other parts of the globe which had fallen under colonial rule at that time it could not stand up. The problem for me was that all the alternative explanations on offer appeared even less convincing.

I continued to struggle with the problem for some time. The equivalent of the undergraduate thesis, the 'special subject' which I opted for under the notable Africanist J. D. Hargreaves was 'the Partition of Africa', and my Ph.D. subject dealt with commercial connections between Glasgow and Africa during the late nineteenth century. In the end, however, not being able to see any solution, I moved my academic interests into other areas of history.

In the following years, however, research, debate and dialogue undertaken both by Marxist and non-Marxist historians has enormously extended the detailed knowledge of what was involved in imperial expansion and consolidation. It has demonstrated, I think beyond argument, that there is no all-encompassing explanation which will account for every territorial extension and every aspect of imperial functioning on the part of Britain, let alone of the entire imperialist system. On the other hand (though there would be no agreement on this) it is my view that it is possible to identify a framework, a model of how the imperial states operated as a global system at this stage of their evolution, which does explain the general drive and outcome of developments. That framework is based upon the concept of 'regimes of accumulation', a modified form of the model propounded by Giovanni Arrighi, as explained in the Introduction to this volume, not forgetting that it was taking place not as a purely economic phenomenon but in a context of competitive power relations between the major states.

However, it has to be emphasised that the concern here is not *primarily* with general theoretical models, but rather with a lower level of particular explanations for more specific developments and outcomes which provides a satisfactory picture of how and why imperial concerns, both formal and informal, became an increasingly important dimension of British public and private life, absorbed so much of political discourse and penetrated so deeply into civil society during the years in question. Chapters 2 and 3 consider how the new British empire of the late nineteenth century, both formal and informal, was acquired, Chapter 4 examines how the parts of the conglomerate, old and new, actually operated, and Chapter 5 considers the political repercussions both for international relations and for British politics.

In addition to an explanatory purpose, this volume is also intended to serve as a reminder. When formal empires were being dismantled, particularly in the early 1960s, imperialism was a politically discredited notion, scorned and repudiated everywhere except the untouchable right, and the imperial powers which tried to hang on to their colonies, such as Portugal, were looked upon as exceptionally reprobate. Of late, however, a retrospective glow of sentiment or even outright endorsement of the imperial era has been observable among right-wing historians and politicians in Britain. The British empire has been validated either explicitly or by implication by historians such as the late Max Beloff. Niall Ferguson has argued that it would have been appropriate to make a deal with the Kaiser in 1914 to ensure its preservation. John Charmley and Alan Clark have advanced similar theses in relation to Hitler in 1940. Even what were formerly regarded on all sides as wholly indefensible imperial regimes have been hotly defended in recent publications, such as by John Cann in relation to Portugal.

This volume is intended to counter any such nostalgia and to make clear the extent to which the British empire (no less than its counterparts) was first and foremost established by predatory methods and designed to fulfil the purposes of the imperial power 'without compassion or compunction' and without regard to the welfare of its subjects (apart from British descended settlers), any benefits accruing to them being incidental by-products. It was a regime, for the non-European populations which fell into its grasp, of terror, oppression, starvation, forced labour, cultural annihilation, degradation and intermittent genocide – and this is not to ignore palliative actions by government officials or missionary bodies, or that 'developmental' gains might also be secured. Nor is it to ignore the fact that there were individuals and organisations in the imperial metropolis combating the imperial drive, but regrettably there is little evidence that they much affected the progress of empire – any more than Noam Chomsky appears to be able to influence the current practices of the US government. It is true that few of the perpetrators were conscious sadists, any more than were mineowners who in the early nineteenth century sent children down the pits, they did what was required of them by the system in which they operated. It is also a truism of historical method that 'the historian is not a judge, still less a hanging judge', and certainly explanation always has to take priority over moral censure. Nevertheless, no reputable historian writes about the workings of the Third Reich without adopting a moral stand-point on the subject and would be rightly condemned if they failed to do so – though of course their position need not be and should not be explic-itly underlined in every paragraph. The British empire, whatever its level of depravity, was not the Third Reich; but the European empires provided the seedbed for the techniques of domination and the attitudes of mind which made the Third Reich possible.[3]

For reasons of space and manageability the focus of this volume is largely confined to the imperial initiatives from the British state and private ad-venturers, relations with rival imperial powers and the imperial culture as it developed within the UK. It discusses too the fate of the victims, but deals only marginally with the context of their pre-colonial past or the resis-tance that they offered to the colonisation process. The nature of those societies was of course portrayed in colonial discourse as repulsive or con-temptible and their human merits dismissed – for example one of the favourite pretexts for territorial seizures in East Africa was to suppress the thriving combined trade in slaves and ivory conducted there by Arab merchants. However, discussion of the pre-colonial societies is an extended and complex field into which it is not possible to enter here.

The great historian Elie Halevy entitled one of the volumes in his 'His-tory of England since 1815' series *Imperialism and the Rise of Labour*. The two items of the title, however, tended to be juxtaposed only in time, for the rise of labour in the late nineteenth and early twentieth centuries did not much impinge on the development of imperialist culture – rather the reverse relationship. Despite the fact that there *were* oppositional organisations and individuals which indicted imperialism, the labour organisations of the time, including the socialist ones, tended to concen-trate upon national perspectives and largely take the empire for granted – where it was discussed it tended to be under the presumption that British tutelage would have to be continued indefinitely, though particular hor-rors might be denounced.[4] Even the international syndicalist movement which emerged in the early years of the twentieth century largely con-fined its attention to white industrial workers. For these reasons British socialism or socialists scarcely feature in this volume. Blindness towards the realities and meaning of imperialism and colonial conquest did in-deed constitute a major gap in the perceptions of the nascent labour move-ment, and one for which it was to pay dearly in subsequent decades – but consideration of that also lies beyond our scope.

I would like to acknowledge the assistance of all who have been concerned in the conception and preparation of this book, but especially the editors at Pluto Press for their long-suffering patience.

Introduction

The late nineteenth-century writings of Joseph Conrad are recognised as being evidently 'imperial novels for imperial times, dealing with the British Empire, its trade and its duties, the crises at its outposts'.[1] The provenance of Conrad's world is clear, the world as seen by the colonising actors. By contrast, colonial imperialism is not generally associated with the nightmare imaginative world of Franz Kafka, which is interpreted above all as supplying a prophetic insight into the European dictatorships of the twentieth century. It only requires a minor shift in perspective, however, to recognise in Kafka's haunted figures the general fate of any member of the subject peoples under imperial rule. 'He became a writer for a new time of darkness.'[2]

The darkness which fell on Europe in the first half of the twentieth century had already descended in the course of former centuries upon other parts of the globe. 'The terrible world of contemporary history' was already being experienced to the full when the twentieth century opened in Africa, India and many other locations. An impenetrable and unintelligible law administered by alien, arbitrary and totally unaccountable bureaucrats, sucking out the life substance and the personal dignity of its victims, summarised the reality encountered by imperial subjects not of European descent – or even ones who were; Latin America was a *locus classicis* for that sort of thing: 'The great labyrinth of arbitrary law, the indifferent officials, the insufficient papers, the hierarchies above hierarchies, the tribunals ... the wait before the door that never opens.'[3] As a writer in the *Cambridge Illustrated History of the British Empire* puts it, a colonial subject learned that 'law consists of the directives of the state and is a prime means of securing its goals and exercising its powers. The colonial period provided no foundation for the use of law by citizens in defence of their rights.'[4]

1

Nature of Empires

Empires of course have remained as a permanent feature of world history since the written record began, and equally certainly the concept has meant very diverse things at different times. Since it attempts to capture a very diffuse reality, the term itself is rather hard to define satisfactorily, but does imply centralised (usually monarchical) power originating in the conquest and exploitation of politically subordinate units (usually of different cultures) and maintained by force. Before the modern period, however, it does not normally include colonisation. The beginning of empire-linked colonial drive from the sixteenth century can be attributed above all to the fact that it became possible for Europeans in centralised states to reach desirable territories outside the Eurasian landmass – the Americas, Australasia and eventually parts of Africa – occupied by inhabitants who could not hope to match European forms of weaponry.

Ancient Empires

The beginnings of literacy coincide with the emergent ancient empires of Babylonia, Egypt, Assyria, to cite only the best remembered, and in the east of the Eurasian continent, the great and remarkably long-lived Han empire of China followed a little later by its Japanese counterpart. The cultural foundations of Europe were laid in the empire established by the Romans and its absorption of Greek and Hellenistic sources (the word 'imperial' itself derives ultimately from ancient Rome). What we classify as the European middle ages (approximately 500–1500 CE) encompassed the Byzantine and Holy Roman empires, the Arab empire and its Turkish successor. Nor were empires by any means confined to the Eurasian landmass – they appear in indigenous sub-Saharan Africa, and famously across the Atlantic in the shape of the Mayan, the Aztec and the Inca examples.

Many of these formations, such as those of the ancient Middle East – or of pre-Colombian America – were little more than tribute-collecting apparatuses which, once having terrorised the subject populations into acquiescence, took them pretty much as they found them. Others like the Roman and Chinese, wholly divergent though these two examples were in their social and economic foundations, had in common the fact that they produced ruling elites who aimed at a significant degree of political cohesion and cultural uniformity.

Medieval Empires

The same was true for medieval Europe in terms of culture, but not political unity, for the Holy Roman empire (roughly modern Germany and Italy), though its emperors had pretensions to exercise a suzerainty over their brother monarchs, could never make that effective. However, medieval western Europe, if it lacked political unity – being split into a collection of mutually hostile kingdoms – possessed a cultural surrogate in the shape of the Roman church. If this polity was materially and culturally less sophisticated than the ancient empires, it was nonetheless technically and economically more dynamic than any previous culture had been. It also reached historically innovative heights of aggressive expansionism. Alien populations on the borders defined as such by their religious difference – Slavs, Estonians, Scandinavians, Moors – were converted, sometimes peacefully, but as often forcibly, to Christendom's cultural norms, the recalcitrant ones exterminated and replaced with settlers drawn from the interior parts of the medieval kingdoms (one of the few examples of pre-modern colonisation in this sense). From all basic agricultural producers, free or serf, a surplus was extracted, which, though initially appropriated by a clerico-military aristocracy, generated impressive economic growth and rapid social transformation. Robert Bartlett ends his comprehensive discussion of the process with the remark that

> Conquest, colonization, Christianization: the techniques of settling in a new land, the ability to maintain cultural identity through legal forms and nurtured attitudes, the institutions and outlook required to confront the strange or abhorrent, to repress it and live with it, the law and religion as well as the guns and ships. The European Christians who sailed to the coasts of the Americas, Asia and Africa in the fifteenth and sixteenth centuries came from a society that was already a colonizing society. Europe, the initiator of one of the world's major processes of conquest, colonization and transformation, was also the product of one.[5]

Although the medieval colonising drive occurred principally on the southern and eastern frontiers of Latin Christendom, a variant of the same process also took place within the British Isles. The date 1066 commemorates the seizure by aggressive Norman-French feudalists of the Anglo-Saxon state and society, which had itself been doing the same kind of thing on the Celtic fringes of the British mainland. 'Internal colonialism' (differing from the modern form in that it did not aim to displace the original

inhabitants but to impose over them a thin stratum of conquering aristo-
crats) extended also to Ireland and continued for centuries to mould the
economic and political features of what would eventually become the
British state.[6]

Modern Empire

What we think of as the modern world was born half a millennium ago in
an act of territorial expansionism when the Genoan adventurer Cristobal
Colomb (Christopher Columbus) pronounced the Caribbean island he
named Hispaniola to be part of the dominions of the Spanish monarchy,
so inaugurating the first of the west European seaborne empires. These were
something genuinely novel and whoever wants to understand the historical trend of the world's development since that time has to keep them in the
foreground, for they were absolutely central. Long-distance commercial
connections overland between Europe, the Middle East and the Asian landmass had existed for centuries, but with the beginnings of American colonisation and the near-simultaneous penetration of European traders down
the African coastline and across the Indian Ocean into southern and eastern Asia, the beginnings of a fully global economy made their appearance,
and may indeed be taken as the defining feature of modernity.

Streams of bullion and exotic plant commodities transformed the commercial economies and through them the state systems of western Europe.[7]
The Anglo-Scottish state formed in the seventeenth and eighteenth centuries was a comparative latecomer to this form of enterprise, but once entered into the contest, and capitalising on resources partly accumulated
from the epoch of internal colonialism, made spectacular progress. South
and Central America were monopolised by the imperialist firstcomers,
Spain and Portugal (though some important Caribbean islands were
snatched from them), but for English colonists having to be content in
the main with the apparently less choice parts of the Americas proved in
the end no disadvantage, for the regions along the North American sea-
board which became the English colonies turned out after all to have greater
economic potential than Mexico or South America, even as pre-industrial
economies.

What the seventeenth century had begun the eighteenth brought to tri-
umphant culmination. A succession of uniformly successful trade and
colonial wars enabled the British agrarian and commercial ruling class[8] to
seize or at least infringe upon the colonial possessions and commerce of
their longer-established state rivals – the Spanish, Portuguese, French and
Dutch. By the 1760s its world trade dominance was assured, backed by a

formidable and virtually unchallengable wooden navy. The prize was control of the commodities which formed the staples of the colonial powers' re-export trades, American sugar, tobacco and coffee, Indian cottons, Chinese tea and silks, East Indian spices.

The first three of these commodities were underpinned by trade of another sort, giving to the Atlantic economy of the eighteenth century the centrality it held for economic and political developments both in Europe and globally. The plantations which produced the coffee, sugar and tobacco of the New World were worked (like the silver mines of the initial colonisation) by forced labour. This labour force was recruited at first from a variety of sources but soon, notoriously, principally from the victims of the West African slave trade – a form of commerce regarded by its practitioners in the same light as any other and before the late eighteenth century looked upon as in no way morally degrading. The unfortunates involved were purchased from local potentates along the African coastline, their acquisition did not require the actual occupation of African territory apart from a few fortified strongholds, and it was none of the business of the slave traders to enquire into their origins or ultimate fate. In this area too British commerce had established its ascendancy by the eighteenth century.[9]

Global Markets by the Eighteenth Century

The global market of the late eighteenth century represented perhaps the pinnacle of commercial development that was possible in a world lacking any significant sources of artificial power and dependent as yet upon wind, water and muscle, human or animal. Its hub was the North Atlantic economy, and the the greater part of the commodities produced by servile labour which were traded across it – sugar, rum, tobacco, coffee, cocoa, cotton fibre – are best classified as semi-luxuries, whose most important role was not as consumption goods in the seaboard states of Europe which imported them (though naturally a portion was used in this fashion) but as re-exports. The spokes radiating out from the hub carried these re-exports to central and southern Europe, the Baltic, what was later to be termed the Middle East, West Africa, southern Asia and China. Along the spokes flowed back timber, hemp, luxury dyestuffs, brassware, wallpaper, finished high-quality cottons, spices, silks, tea, porcelain.

Primitive Capital Accumulation

It would, of course, be wrong to envisage merchant capital and commercial imperialism as a deliberately planned regime of primitive accumulation for the Industrial Revolution[10] which began to develop as the eigh-teenth-century empire attained its apogee – any more than the canal net-work was intended as a preliminary sketch for the succeeding railway system. Nevertheless, it is safe to say that without the existence of that imperial foundation the industrialisation process would have been at least much retarded and more likely aborted altogether. Slave merchants from Bristol financed mining and ironwork ventures in south Wales; their Liverpool counterparts did the same thing for Lancashire cotton. Glasgow merchants grown wealthy on tobacco imports provided the capital for Clydeside textiles. Indian bullion manured the spreading undergrowth of private banks in England. Above all, the slave labour force imported ini-tially to North America to grow tobacco could be adapted to cultivate the vegetable fibre central to the initial phase of industrialisation – raw cot-ton. The political secession of the North American colonies in the shape of the United States involved for a long time no basic alteration in eco-nomic relationships.[11]

Regimes of Accumulation

Between its initial formation at the end of the fifteenth century and the advanced state of development achieved three hundred years later, the glo-bal economy continued to be based upon regimes of plunder, unashamedly unequal exchange and forced labour. From that era of primary accumula-tion 'dripping with blood and dirt from every pore', in Marx's words,[12] the world economy perpetually expanded, consolidated and institutionalised itself, and also underwent a process of constant transmogrification – though it did not cease either to drip with blood and dirt.

In fact it passed through several 'regimes of accumulation' as I will term them, and each of these discrete stages of development was also politically structured. The essence of that structure was a central economy based in one particular state whose owners of capital were thereby enabled to domi-nate the circuits of global exchange in whatever form they assumed at particular historical times.[13] In the original manifestation it was the Span-ish monarchy (which was not geographically confined to Spain) control-ling the flow of bullion across the Atlantic, together with the import of spices from eastern Asia and European commerce from its Netherlands and Italian bases.

The second phase or regime of accumulation runs from the middle of the seventeenth to the early nineteenth century. It incorporated within itself the older form as a subordinate element, but was more specifically characterised by a world commerce in the semi-luxuries noted above –

tobacco, sugar, Indian cottons, Chinese silks and tea, South American coffee – as well as plantation slavery and an element of trade relations with
the ancient empires of Turkey, China and Mughal India. With the Spanish
monarchy decrepit, it took time to settle which of the European states would
dominate the new structure, for it was a bitterly fought struggle between
three contenders – the Dutch Republic, which had seceded from the Spanish empire, France and England (or, more accurately, the Anglo-Scottish
state). The Dutch were the first to drop out and accept a secondary position, not having the size, production or population resources to sustain a
conflict lasting a century and a half. England (now transformed into Britain) and France continued to sustain the contest throughout the course of
the eighteenth and early nineteenth century, with Britain in the more
advantageous position, until in 1815 it emerged as the clear winner, its
decisive advantages being superior financial management and naval firepower.

Even as this definitive supremacy was gained, the global economy and
the character of the seaborne empires which dominated it, above all the
British, stood upon the brink of a further fundamental change. Machine
industry had reached the stage of development where, manifested especially in railway systems, it was about to rise as the dominant sector in the
economies of western European states and the USA and profoundly affect
their relations with the remainder of the world. Closely tied in with this
phase of world market expansion and transformation, territorial imperialism attained its zenith by the end of the century, when scarcely any
portion of the world's surface was not subjected to the political hegemony
of one of the western nations, either directly as a colony or else controlled
informally.

The history of imperial relationships between the powers, considered
as an interlocking developing system, is an area which merits extensive
study. In this short volume however, though that is touched upon where
necessary, the focus is upon the British part of the structure, and indeed
upon its culminating phase of territorial acquisition, the years between
1870 and 1914.[14]

Industrial Economy

By the middle of the nineteenth century, machine industry with its associated transport and extractive systems had become the dominant sector of
the British economy and for two decades or more it was in the unique
position of being the only industrial economy in a world of agrarian trading partners, or ones still struggling to find their way along the industrial

route. The strength and self-confidence of the country's industrial bour-geoisie, and the governments which responded to their importunities[15] was exhibited in the dogma of free trade – a reflection of the superiority of British manufactures and British commercial enterprise over all rivals, the presumption that in an open market, rather than the protected ones which had characterised the eighteenth and first part of the nineteenth century, British entrepreneurs would invariably win.

Yet empire had by no means disappeared – in fact it had expanded. In terms of geographical extent the Canadian territories, various West Indian islands, Australasia, Cape Colony, together with the major part of the Indian subcontinent, subjugated after 1800 – not directly by the British state but by a chartered commercial company with delegated powers – were considerably bigger than the thirteen American colonies lost in 1783 and in terms of population immensely more so. At the mid-point of the nineteenth century they fulfilled a set of divergent roles, very different from the colonial structure of the previous century and very different again from those which they would assume within only another twenty years. Most of them served functions that might or might not be enhanced by their colonial relationship: whether as sources of cane sugar or dumping grounds for convicts. For most of these areas, however, it would not have made any crucial difference to the British economy if they had been outside British government control.

The exception was India, where it would have made a very substantial difference indeed even apart from the regulated plunder extracted by the East India Company through the state powers conferred upon it – a major component in City transactions. Following the secession of the North American colonies 'the empire became for the most part a system of rule over non-European peoples. Its centre of gravity would be the Indian Ocean rather than the Atlantic.'[16] Without the enormous Indian export market, protected in reality if not in form from foreign competition, Lancashire cotton manufacture, the very pivot of industrialisation, would have been effectively crippled. The destruction of the handicraft cotton manufactures of Bengal, as the local market was flooded with machine-produced tex-tiles, with consequent mass starvation,[17] had been the precondition for the final mechanisation and rapid growth of the Lancashire industry ear-lier in the century. India's subject status fulfilled an additional important function: the subcontinent furnished the necessary base for the penetra-tion of East Asian commerce, particularly the Chinese market. The com-modity which in this case provided the cutting edge of commercial pen-etration was opium – produced and exported from India and forced upon the Chinese at gunpoint.

Capital Investment and Industrial Challenge

Overlapping although not wholly coinciding with the above development, the City since 1815, capitalising on techniques evolved during the French Wars, had begun to experiment with the export of capital, the practice of foreign investment, through loans to foreign governments, investment in canal construction in the USA or, tentatively, mining and agricultural enterprises. A lot of capital was thus sunk in the 1820s and 1830s, and (in Eric Hobsbawm's words) much of it was sunk without trace, but the experience provided valuable training for what was to come. By the date of the Great Exhibition of 1851 Britain was unquestionably an industrial economy and the 1850s and 1860s marked the era of its apparently unchallengable ascendancy both industrially and commercially. Nevertheless, by the early 1870s the position was changing and the unchallengeable was about to be challenged.

Second Industrial Revolution – the Global Economy 1870–1914

In the course of the 1870s a number of developments – in technology, raw material inputs, trade and consumption patterns, agriculture, population movements, price levels, capital flows – came together to produce what economic historians often refer to as 'the second industrial revolution'. Technological innovation affected both existing technologies, and more importantly, produced an entire new range. Steam engines and steel production methods were revolutionised, as were certain textile manufacturing processes. Industrial chemistry entered a new era. Even more significant, however, was the emergence of new power sources in the form of the petrol engine and electricity with its multitude of possible applications; communications in a variety of dimensions from telephones and the sound phonograph to the motor vehicle and cinematography. The new commodities and processes demanded on a hitherto unprecedented scale access to a range of raw materials such as copper, rubber (essential both in tyres and for insulating electrical cables and wires) and above all, as the years advanced, oil. In all the developed countries, but particularly the United States and Germany (Britain was less affected, but did not escape the process) there emerged on an unprecedented scale cartels and giant quasi-monopolies controlling large sectors of production and the domestic market, and in Germany a growing coalescence between banking and industrial capital. The global character of these developments was underlined by the phenomenal leap which occurred in the export of capital, funds seeking profitable investment opportunities abroad from the economies of Britain, Germany and France.

The industrialisation of the United States was beginning to get into its stride and its domestic market was starting to feel a decreasing need for British capital goods, although it was to remain for many years a voracious importer of British funds. In central Europe the establishment of the German Reich created a direct competitor in world export markets,[18] a formidable trading rival whose industrial structure and technology was in many respects ahead of the British.[19] The arrival of intensified competition throughout the world economy was signalled by the long-term price deflation and reduced growth rates labelled the 'great Victorian depression', which in spite of its name, did not affect Britain only. The unity of the world economy remained – was drawn tighter indeed – but at the same time subjected to developing strains and tensions.

Unstable Structure

Simultaneously, the diplomatic process was initiated which over forty years divided the major states of Europe between two hostile camps armed to the teeth. Whether this was the cause or the consequence of commercial and investment rivalries and competitive empire-building is not our immediate concern – the argument is a complex one – but undeniably the two processes were closely related and by the early twentieth century the European states and their direct and indirect dependencies, together with the United States, formed a complex and diversified but highly unstable interlocking structure of wealth and power. Within this, the British imperial system constituted the central element. Its formal empire was the biggest of any, its shipping dominated the commercial sea-lanes as its warfleet did the strategic harbours and communications. It overshadowed all rivals in the provision of commercial and financial services, its currency served as the world standard of value, its overseas investments eclipsed those of any competitor. These realities had profound implications for the character of class relations, ideological perceptions and political interactions within the British Isles themselves.

Lenin's Interpretation[20]

By far the most influential interpretation of the global imperialist process was, as noted in the preface, that sketched by Lenin in 1916, which attributed the development to a mutation within world capitalism. According to this model, tendencies towards the replacement of open markets by monopoly control, combined with greater profits to be earned from investment abroad, induced capital to mobilise the power of governments to divide and redivide the world into exclusive zones of interest, often but not invariably taking the shape of formal colonies. He summarised it as follows:

> Imperialism is capitalism in that stage of development in which the domination of the monopolies and finance capital has established itself; in which the export of capital has acquired pronounced importance; in which the division of the world among the international trusts has begun; in which the partition of all the territories of the globe among the great capitalist powers has been completed.[21]

In this manner, the outbreak of the European conflict in 1914 is also explained as a general struggle for redivision of the territorial and economic loot once there were no unclaimed portions remaining, and the collapse of the established European labour movements into chauvinism and 'sacred union' with their rulers on the commencement of the war was accounted for by their leaders having been bribed out of imperial super-profits.[22]

For over thirty years a sustained historiographical attack was deployed against this thesis – its beginning coinciding, and probably not accidentally, with when the rate of African decolonisation was gathering pace in the early 1960s. The effect of this revision, whatever the intention (and no-one need impugn the motives of the academics in question) would be to acquit capitalism, whose future on the continent was then at stake, of the crimes of imperialism, for which few by then had a good word – all of which does not necessarily invalidate the rebuttal of Lenin's thesis: the evidence has to be considered on its merits, and the evidence, as suggested above, is adverse to Lenin, at least in so far as tropical colonies are concerned.

The present text will not address that debate in great detail, though a full accounting for late nineteenth-century imperialism must certainly engage with it and it is hoped that a subsequent volume will explore the full range of theoretical issues with reference to such authors as, inter alia Fieldhouse, Robinson and Gallagher, Offer, Platt, O'Brien, Cain and Hopkins. Nonetheless, in this more modest project of identifying the forces and processes which propelled the world's most advanced industrial nation, already possessed of a substantial empire, into participation in a further climactic spasm of colony-seizure, an explanatory model is of course unavoidable, both for the general course of imperialism during the last half-millennium and more specifically the form which it assumed from around 1870.

The pre-industrial version of world supremacy had required colonies, settlements and dependencies as subordinate producers and part of its control mechanisms. Mid-nineteenth-century capital and its spokespersons were inclined to wonder whether it could not dispense with the cost of those it had inherited from the former era and rely altogether on the invisible empire outlined above, with the British Navy placed discreetly in the background.

It was bound to be a historically transient state of affairs (though I think it might have lasted somewhat longer than it did) and before long capital centred in other European states and in the USA, and obliged on pain of perpetual subordination to try to copy the British achievement had succeeded in doing so. In certain respects, exploiting superior technology and economies of scale, their industrialists before the end of the century significantly surpassed their British counterparts, who nevertheless continued to dominate the global circuits. As these circuits expanded to hitherto untouched areas and deepened in complexity, the German state, the most successful of the new industrial powers, conceived hegemonic aims which eventually brought it into direct conflict with its British predecessor. Even before that point was reached, however, the repercussions of the German geopolitical impact on Europe, together with the politically fragmented and 'primitive' character of the new areas to which capital was extending its reach, had occasioned the addition between 1880 and 1900 of an extended territorial empire to the invisible one already noted.

Thus was born the new imperialism. My argument will be that the overt acquisition of new dependencies in the late nineteenth century represented only a part, and not necessarily even the most significant part, of that reality. By 1914 virtually all the territorial disputes which these scrambles generated had been settled diplomatically, but the military blocs formed around the two rival claimants to global hegemony nevertheless clashed in an annihilating conflict which thoroughly destabilised and partially destroyed the structures of both the world economy and international state system. To look for a moment beyond the limits of our study, British capital found the fruits of its apparent triumph in 1918 exceedingly sour ones, and it was clear that by then an even more threatening rival to its hegemony, such as it was, over the crippled world trade system had appeared in the shape of the USA. The general economic breakdown, however, postponed for twenty years realisation of the US potential, while German capital, organised by a terrorist and psychopathic regime, tried once more between 1938 and 1945 to assert world supremacy. The outcome of *that* conflict left the City in unquestionable if reluctant subordination to the dollar and the USA exercising, except over the communist bloc, the same kind of financial authority that Britain had done half a century before-hand.

Scope of Discussion

Chapter 1 considers the antecedents of the concept of imperialism and the background of developments in the British Isles which turned England/Britain into the most successful of commercial imperialist states by the eighteenth century and the hub of a world exchange system, and reviews the position reached by the middle of the nineteenth century and the colonial empire acquired up to that point, while Chapter 2 examines in more detail the character and structural importance of these colonies on the eve of the great expansion, together with the internal forces in British politics and society reformulating and promoting the imperial idea.

Chapters 3 to 5 cover the course of colonial acquisition, examine how the imperial system worked in practice from the point of view of both colonisers and colonised, and discuss the impact of these events on social relations in Britain, high and popular culture and the shape imposed upon the country's political evolution. External political relations are discussed in terms of goals and motives impelling the diplomatic manoeuvres and eventual military clash of rival empires. Chapter 6 makes an attempt to sum up and evaluate the significance for the British people, and particularly of the labour movement, of this imperialist phase and indicate its long-term historical legacy down to the present.

Further Reading

Perry Anderson, 'Origins of the Present Crisis', *New Left Review* 23, Jan/Feb 1964. A classic overview of British capitalism from the revolution of the seventeenth century onwards.

Emannuel Arrighi, *The Long Twentieth Century*, Verso, 1994. Covers an even lengthier span. Demanding, but very rewarding.

Robert Bartlett, *The Making of Europe*, Penguin, 1993. Medieval colonialism.

Ben Brewer, *Marxist Theories of Imperialism*, Routledge and Kegan Paul, 1980.

Michael Hechter, *Internal Colonialism*, Routledge and Kegan Paul, 1975. Deals with early-modern colonial expansion in the British Isles.

E.J. Hobsbawm, *The Age of Capital 1848–1875*, Weidenfeld & Nicolson, 1975. Classic overview of world history during these years.

E.J. Hobsbawm, *The Age of Empire 1875–1914*, Weidenfeld & Nicolson, 1987. Covers both the growth of empires and the forces which motivated it.

Tom Kemp, *Industrialisation in Nineteenth-century Europe*, Longman, 1969.

Tom Kemp, *Theories of Imperialism*, Dennis Dobson, 1967. Marxist theories from a Trotskyist perspective.

V.G. Kiernan, *Marxism and Imperialism*, Edward Arnold, 1974. A set of scintillating essays.

V.I. Lenin, *Imperialism: The Highest Stage of Capitalism*, 1916 (*Collected Works*, vol. 22, Lawrence & Wishart, 1964). The classic Marxist interpretation.

R. Owen and B. Sutcliffe, *Studies in the Theory of Imperialism*, Longman, 1972. A very wide-ranging discussion.

1

The British Empire on the Eve

The British empire, acquired in stages since the seventeenth century, had by 1870 already reached a size both in area and population greater than any of its rivals were to attain by 1914. The oldest components consisted of Bermuda and a large number of West Indian islands, of which Jamaica was the biggest, though not as large as the South American mainland colony, British Guiana. These represented an important but far from central element in the imperial structure.

The settlement colonies, whose name indicates their essential character, were Canada, Australia (until 1900 seven separate colonies) and New Zealand, to which should be added the South African possessions of Cape Colony and Natal, different from the others because British-descended settlers could never hope to form a majority of their population. The 'jewel in the crown' was of course India, with its enormous wealth, indigenous population and high civilisation, conquered piece by piece since the 1750s. The conquest of Ceylon to the south and Burma to the east had reflected the same process on a lesser scale.

The remainder of the empire, though amounting to a considerable population overall, represented only dots and patches upon the map – such as the Central American colony of British Honduras, Gibraltar, Malta, Heligoland, the Ionian Islands, the Gambia, a strip of the later Sierra Leone, several forts on the West African Gold Coast, a scattering of South Atlantic islands, footholds on the coast of the Malay peninsula and East Indies, and Hong Kong, forcibly leased from the Chinese authorities.

These constituted the formal empire. The 'informal empire' over which the British state and/or capital exercised a greater or lesser hegemony included the republics of South America and the decaying empires of the Turkish and Persian sovereigns.

The Background

British global policy in the mid-nineteenth century has been termed 'the imperialism of free trade',[1] and the designation contains a great measure of truth. Even before free trade was a fully-fledged reality, Marx observed percipiently in the *Communist Manifesto*: 'The cheap prices of [the bourgeoisie's] commodities are the heavy artillery with which it batters down all Chinese walls, with which it forces the barbarians' intensely obstinate hatred of foreigners to capitulate.'[2] Around that point in time a regime of global accumulation still basically agricultural and underpinned by natural power sources – wind, water and above all human muscle – was in transition to one dependent upon the artificial power of steam, which was technologically developed and industrial in the modern sense of the term. Uniquely in these transitions, the same society and state which had presided over the previous form, which had reached its apogee in the late eighteenth century, was also the centre of the new one.

The British economy depended upon global markets and it was export-dependent to an extraordinary degree. British industrial products dominated the circuits of global exchange; the Great Exhibition of 1851 was a demonstration and celebration of that ascendancy – and yet was only a foretaste of what was to follow in the next two decades. Free trade was the instrument through which these markets were protected and expanded. In form free trade, as expounded by its partisans such as Richard Cobden, represented a regime of equality founded upon the doctrine of comparative cost advantage – every part of the world complex of production and exchange would produce whatever it was best fitted to, and thereby establish its superiority in that particular line of production. Free trade would act as the invisible hand deterring countries or regions from trying to enter inappropriate lines; it would compel them to maximise their natural advantages and make every part of the world mutually dependent – generating international concord and amity as welcome by-products.

The reality, it need hardly be stressed, was very different. The doctrine of comparative advantage assumed static conditions, it took no account of development over time and the conditions it assumed were those of the mid-nineteenth century, in which Britain (by following an earlier policy of protectionism) had got the edge, and in most cases much more than the edge, over every other country in industrial production. By the early 1850s the UK was effectively (ignoring points of detail) the sole industrialised country in a non-industrialised world, which gave it command over global markets both as an exporter and importer. Free trade, in other words, was the ideological sanctification for British industrial, commercial and financial ascendancy.

The Global Economy and the Empire

In the two decades following 1850 the relationship of Britain to its trading partners, and particularly to its formal and informal dependencies, was transformed. The agent of transformation was the railway and in two dimensions its consequences were momentous. The development of this transport system, combined with steam ocean navigation, which doubled its efficiency in the 1850s,[3] not to speak of the telegraph, abolished distance and inaccessibility, brought within reach of the market bulk mineral and agricultural commodities on a hitherto unimaginable scale – US wheat, Chilean copper, Australian wool, eventually Argentinian beef and New Zealand mutton, to mention only some particularly notable examples. The other principal feature of worldwide railway construction was the scope which it provided for large-scale investment in foreign parts – a form of enterprise which, through this medium, British capital now started to address in a serious fashion – exporting not only the funds but often the rails, equipment, rolling stock and labour force as well.[4] Further investment could then follow to develop the mines, ranches or plantations which the railway made viable. In the later nineteenth century the railway was the key to political and economic success in the settlement colonies. At the time a colonial or subordinate relationship on the part of the recipient was hardly needed to facilitate the process, as nobody else was exporting railways. Lending by British investors to foreign governments also resumed on a large scale during these two decades.

In short, what had been for over a century a global economy in terms of trade networks, became an enormously more tightly articulated and productive one. While this was happening in the course of the 1850s and 1860s there was little extension of formal colonies on the part of any European power.[5] Thanks to new technologies and opportunities, however, fresh potential could be perceived and developed in ones which had been appropriated by European states for a variety of purposes in an earlier economic era, while the ongoing penetration of weaker and technically less developed extra-European economies eroded the latters' stability and autonomy. Dominating the entire structure were British production, British commerce and British financial services, and, it might be added, British economic ideology, as free markets and free trade came to be perceived as the wave of the future by enlightened opinion throughout the 'civilised' world.[6]

Not surprisingly in such circumstances the continuing need for colonies was called into question; the existing ones appeared to add little to such already overwhelming dominance. What the participants had in mind during such discussions was in the main what would be called the settlement colonies, with the envisaged model being the United States. James Stephen, the civil servant who dominated British colonial administration from the 1820s to 1847, regarded their existence as a misfortune for Britain which had to be patiently borne until the settlers decided for themselves to end the connection. There did exist in the 1830s and 1840s a group of upper-middle-class publicists who proposed a diametrically opposite view and in some measure prefigured the notions of Joseph Chamberlain at the end of the century: they advocated a doctrine of 'systematic colonisation' and settlement of the colonies as one component of an authoritarian social programme also embracing Britain. Their leading spokesperson was Edward Gibbon Wakefield, who founded the National Colonisation Society (and was ridiculed by Marx in an appendix to the first volume of *Capital*).

The most important of all the imperial possessions was not really thought of as a colony. India was a conglomeration of territories ruled formally or informally by a commercial enterprise, the East India Company, though that had demitted its commercial functions in 1833 to concentrate upon raising revenue from taxation. The subcontinent was of the utmost commercial importance to Britain and British policy was consistently aggressive – politically, territorially and culturally. In the words of General Sir Charles Napier, conqueror of Sind, and intimidator of Chartists:

> Would I were king of India! I would make Moscowa and Pekin shake ... England's fleet should be all in the west and the Indian army all in the east. India ... should suck English manufactures up her great rivers, and pour down those rivers her own varied products.[7]

Which certainly has the virtue of expressing concisely the relationship between geopolitics, military power and commercial aspiration. In the more sober terminology two present-day historians:

> From the 1850s India became a notable outpost of the new service and financial order which had come to prominence in Britain following the demise of Old Corruption and sterling's role as a world currency. The main instruments of British policy in India, the army and civil service employed only a small number of white officials. But they had their hands on the levers of power: they controlled the means of coercion,

they collected and allocated India's vast revenues, and their values helped to shape policy and its execution ... the Indian army remained vital to Britain's presence in Asia, both for reasons of internal security and for policing the vast region stretching from the Eastern Mediterranean to China. Without the Indian Army and the Indian revenues that sustained it, Britain would not have been able to maintain her position east of Suez, and her status as a great power would have been seriously impaired.[8]

From time to time the Company and government authorities in London would object to the annexationist activities of their proconsuls in India (usually on grounds of cost) but always ended up endorsing them. This too set a precedent for what was to occur several decades later in tropical Africa.

Free trade, whatever its theoretical aspirations, was in the real world, and not only in India, far from being a harbinger of peace and co-operation. In relation to countries recognised as forming part of the concert of nations and disposing of significant military forces the missionaries of free trade had to proceed by negotiation and diplomacy. Elsewhere, however, if the barbarians were so retarded as to stay unimpressed by the cheapness of British commodities, punitive force, with or without subsequent annexation, was always at hand to bring them to their senses.

So it was employed against the Burmese kings, commencing in 1824 and continuing until 1852, with their territory annexed to the Indian empire, but the most dramatic instance of this aspect of the imperialism of free trade was seen in the wars waged against the Chinese Empire from the late 1830s to the late 1850s. These conflicts had a variety of pretexts but the essential purpose was in every case the same – to compel the Chinese authorities to reverse their attempts to regulate trading relations in the Chinese ports and instead permit into the Celestial empire the import of opium cultivated in British India – for this drug was the mainstay of the far eastern trade and without it the British merchant houses had no commodity which was in great demand in the Chinese market, while the abolition in 1833 of the East India Company's monopoly of trade with China sharpened their appetites. Following the first of the Opium Wars in 1839 the territory of Hong Kong was secured to make the trade easier to conduct, though in deference to China's nominal recognition as a state it was 'leased' rather than annexed outright.

In this manner China began its career as the most striking instance of a development originating in the first half of the century, pioneered in London, and destined to a long and discreditable career – the informal or semi-colony, in which ostensibly sovereign states were induced by diplomatic pressure or, as in the Chinese case, armed coercion to modify their external trade relations so as to give British commercial entrepreneurs a free hand, enabling them to convert these polities into economic colonies and even to determine the direction of their productive activity. Along with China[9] such a fate had also overtaken the politically decaying, feudally structured Ottoman empire and the weak successor states to the Spanish empire in South America, particularly its southern cone.

British Society

The third quarter of the nineteenth century formed a watershed not only in the economic history of the UK but in its social and political relations as well. In general terms it represented a recrystallisation of social and class structures after the tectonic shifts and eruptions of the Industrial Revolution. The manual workforce, whether or not employed in technologically advanced industry, adapted to the reality and permanence of industrial society or sought better prospects overseas. As Edward Thompson put it, they 'proceeded to warren it from end to end ... the characteristic class institutions of the Labour Movement were built up – trade unions, trades councils, TUC, co-ops and the rest – which have endured to this day'.[10]

The propertied (except for occasional brief panics) no longer lived in fear of the mob. The revolution in Paris on February 1848 had profoundly alarmed the authorities in London, in real fear of a British imitation; the Paris Commune of 1871 (much though British elites deplored it) did not. These years saw a consolidation of the social structures formed in the matrix of the previous six decades and the emergence of many other institutions – from universities and the banking system to sports clubs – in the form which in essence they retain to this day. The propertied class had changed in composition and character, so had the ranks of the propertyless, and compared with the turmoils of the first half of the century general stability marked the structure which had evolved.

In certain respects there was melioration. Both the agricultural and industrial economies stabilised. In spite of occasional tremors there was to be in the 1850s to 1870s nothing like the roller-coaster experience of boom and slump of the earlier decades or the chronic recession which set in after 1873. Albeit marginally and slowly, real incomes improved, as did general standards of diet. The first moves were initiated towards effective urban sanitation and lighting, pure water supply, public health. What would become known in later times as the 'trickle-down' theory of allocation appeared to work marvellously and free trade concepts appeared to be eminently justified.

Political change followed. The struggle by the propertyless in the form of the Chartist movement to break directly into the electoral arena had been decisively repulsed, but the pressure for a widened franchise continued in a lower key through a variety of ad hoc associations. In 1867 a combination of these pressures with political opportunism on the part of the Conservative parliamentary leadership produced the Second Reform Act, instituting an approximation to a household franchise in the urban areas. The expansion of the electorate thus produced had considerable implications for political management.

Belligerent xenophobia and conviction of national superiority had been for more than two centuries a central component of English popular culture, generated firstly by the internal colonialism of the early modern era in relation to Scotland and Ireland, and more importantly by the century-long cycle of trade wars with France, of which the final episode, ending in 1815, had also been a counter-revolutionary war. It was this feature of the national psyche that Lord Palmerston had been so adept at playing upon during the middle years of the century to mobilise popular support for aggressions committed under the banner of free trade. It was reinforced (with comparable developments in Scotland) by the influx of Irish immigration from the 1840s onward. As circumstances changed after the early 1870s this sense of national superiority was ready and waiting for exploitation by demagogues, politicians, journalists and the would-be empire-builders who then made their entrance upon the historical stage.

Prelude

In the second half of the nineteenth century a substantial flow of voluntary emigrants left Britain for permanent settlement overseas.[11] The most common destination, it is true, was the United States, but considerable numbers also ended up in Canada and Australia, while South Africa and New Zealand, though less popular, attracted enough to fix these areas of settlement as part of a global network of English-speaking communities. The process resulted in the cases of Canada and Australia in the marginalisation or near extermination of the indigenous population – through massacre, disease, alcoholism, depressed birth rates – and in South Africa and New Zealand to its dispossession and complete subordination.

What these colonies had in common, the feature which provided the attraction for immigrants, was that for the most part they lay within the temperate zones of the northern or southern hemispheres, and therefore possessed, once the obstacle of their original inhabitants was removed, great potential for variants of British agricultural practice,[12] and, with cheap land and economies of scale, the potential for exploiting British consumer demand. However, it was a potential only realisable for the most part by means of steam-driven transport systems and, ultimately, refrigeration and therefore it was not until the 1870s that the settlement colonies began to develop as part of a coherent producing, trading and financial complex centred on the UK. To simplify somewhat, the role that these territories fulfilled was essentially that of agricultural extensions to the British economy, significantly reducing the prices of certain raw materials, particularly wool and, slightly later, foodstuffs, upon the British market, a feature that had implications for class relations and social stability within the UK, for it meant that the masses could enjoy rising standards of consumption without too seriously depressing British profit margins as a result. Within their own boundaries these colonies erected superstructures of transport, construction, service industries, administration and land speculation upon the agricultural foundation.

All of these developments as they accelerated in the last third of the century – agricultural development, ongoing railway and harbour construction, building, civil engineering, mining where it occurred, and the service activities – required funding and thereby, since they mostly enjoyed social and political conditions which minimised risk, provided attractive opportunities for British investors. Faced with large debt repayments, while waiting for the returns on the investments to come on stream, the settlement colonies frequently experienced adverse balance of payments *vis-à-vis* the UK, requiring further lending to plug the gap. The City and the circles of finance capital provided much but by no means all of the funding. The savings of the lower middle classes were tapped as well through the mechanism of the investment trust, institutions which relieved the individual investor of having to make particular decisions about where to invest and which guaranteed (or purported to do so) to bring in the best and safest returns with the funds entrusted to them. They reached a far wider public than the stock exchange, both socially and geographically: a major centre was in fact the city of Dundee.

The settlement colonies were thus tightly bound into an economic system centred on the UK market and controlled by its financial apparatus. They were no less tightly integrated into a seaborne military structure equipped for defensive or offensive action on behalf of British interests anywhere in the world. The colonies' white male inhabitants nevertheless enjoyed a good deal of local political autonomy which it was thought safe and expedient to concede on account of the transplanted British commercial and cultural values with which they operated.[13] Each of these colonies possessed an elected assembly which, under the supervision of a British-appointed governor, handled internal colonial affairs, particularly the procedures for land allocation.

In Australasia, especially, land was cheap while skilled labour was scarce and expensive. Consequently, the political profile, not to mention the earnings, of the white manual workforce were raised above those of their counterparts anywhere in the contemporaneous world; labour parties developed and commitments to measures of social welfare were placed on the political agenda a decade and more before similar developments in the UK. A more sinister aspect of the process, however, was the determination of the British-descended labour force to protect its favoured position in the labour market by excluding on racist criteria the immigration of potentially cheaper labour from Asia – an attitude and practice embodied in the 'White Australia' policy.

In South Africa wholly different circumstances existed due to the potential availability of a black helot reservoir of unskilled labour and the shift in the balance of the region's economy from agriculture to diamonds and gold. Even so, commencing from a different starting point the outcome was in certain respects a similar one and attitudes of racial exclusiveness among white skilled workers, coupled with a rhetoric of social radicalism, emerged, particularly within the mining industry.

The settlement colonies then, quite apart from the later central importance of South African gold, served as important elements in the British global economic network as suppliers of foodstuffs and raw materials, as markets for British industrial products, as outlets for emigration and as absorbers of capital; but it has to be noted that in all these respects they were eclipsed by a politically independent entity, namely the United States. The USA was not, like the settlement colonies, merely a supplementary supplier of foodstuffs to British consumers: by the late 1980s its grain exports had ruined English arable farming. It took more exports and more immigrants than any other part of the world. The expansion of its population and the pace of its agricultural and industrial growth made it a voracious consumer of capital and although most of that country's investment was domestically generated there was plenty of scope for the City and the investment trusts as well.[14] In short, from a purely economic point of view the United States during the late nineteenth century fulfiled the same role as the settlement colonies, only more so. The main difference from the British point of view was that it did not provide administrative posts or sinecures for the British ruling class and did not constitute part of its global military network.

India

The position of India was unique. Its role as the base for far eastern trade has been noted, and it grew the opium which initially prised open that market. As an absorber of exports and capital it was overshadowed only by the United States; as a generator of revenues it had no equal. It produced cotton, sugar cane, indigo and jute among other critically important British imports. The taxes exacted by the Indian government – exacted for the most part ultimately from subsistence peasant farmers and resulting in growing levels of famine in the course of the nineteenth century – sustained the remittances on government borrowing and the parasitic bureaucracy through which the subcontinent was administered, up to 1858 by the East India Company and thereafter directly by the British crown.[15] It also sustained the Indian army, which represented the largest land force available to the British state and was critically important not only for internal policing and tax collection but served as the mainstay, alongside the navy, of British power from China to the Middle East. More than any other part of the empire, India had been and remained fundamental to the concerns of the British ruling class. Lord Salisbury referred to it as 'an English barrack in the Oriental Seas'.[16]

The Caribbean islands, small in geographical extent, had been a central component of the eighteenth-century empire as the source of the immensely valuable cane sugar crop – and important too for the rum distilled from it. In the nineteenth century, if less crucial to the structure of trade as colonial re-exports from Britain to its overseas markets were superseded by manufactures, the islands, together with the colony of British Guiana on the South American mainland, nevertheless remained significant as producers of that commodity, whose centrality to British social life can scarcely be over rated and which constituted an important energy source for the labouring population. Since the 1830s the plantations had ceased to be cultivated by slave labour but were instead tended by the descendants of the slave population as a propertyless free labour force which could be expanded or contracted according to the labour demands of the cycle of cane cultivation.[17] On top of this basic class division rested a complex hierarchy of status differentials associated with degree of skin pigmentation. In 1864 social protest in the oldest Caribbean colony, Jamaica, had escalated into an insurrection, suppressed with relentless ferocity by the authorities and the British military, the suppression being applauded by many of the great and the good within the British Establishment.[18]

At the beginning of the 1870s the only large British possession in Africa was the agricultural settlement colony and key to the Pacific sea-route a the Cape, but certain other bridgeheads did exist. These were located along the coastline west of the Niger and had their origin from the earlier decades of the century as bases for naval action to suppress the West African slave trade following the abandonment by the British of this form of commerce and its outlawing by international agreement. The Liverpool slaving firms had meantime switched their activities into 'legitimate commerce' and found a commodity on which to reconstitute their fortunes, the vegetable oil produced in the Niger delta, which they purchased through the same local rulers that had formerly been their suppliers of slaves, and in this they managed perfectly adequately without any need for an imperial presence. Indeed, by the 1860s the West African outposts were regarded in government circles as of such negligible importance that it was seriously proposed to abandon them.

The 1870s

The 1870s marked a turning point in a number of dimensions for Britain, Europe and the wider world. Economically, steam transport enhanced the flexibility of the global market and technological growth brought new industrial economies onto the scene, resulting in long-term deflation of prices and profits, more stringent competition and rising tariff barriers. Socially and politically, labour movements in a number of European countries constituted organisations and parties which began to assert demands for political power or even threaten revolution. Diplomatically and militarily, the processes got underway which culminated in the division of Europe into two antagonistic armed blocs.

So far as Britain was concerned, a spatter of still relatively minor colonial wars and expansions occurred on the frontiers of its existing empire, principally in Africa. More important was the creation of a sentiment, a reorientation of public attitudes towards openly imperialistic ambitions, an acceptance and expectation which penetrated deep into British society, that the empire was worth preserving, consolidating and expanding. A precursor of what was to come was the two-volume text *Greater Britain* (the title is eloquent enough) published by the rising Liberal politician Sir Charles Dilke. Containing phrases such as 'America, Australia, India, must form a Greater Britain' and 'the difficulties which impede the progress to universal dominion of the English people lie in the conflict with the cheaper races', the book made a considerable impact. The date was 1868.

The ideological foundations were being laid for the annexations and colony-seizure that was to follow, with Africa as the principal theatre. In 1872 the British agent Sir Bartle Frere coerced the Arab Sultan of Zanzibar, ruler of a trading empire that had in 1832 shifted its base from the Oman and the nominal overlord of wide domains in East Africa, into putting his signature to a treaty that ostensibly prohibited slave trading within his territories. The question of that commerce and the difficulty of extirpating it by diplomatic or informal means was to be made into a favourite piece of rhetoric employed by the interests promoting commercial penetration and territorial takeover in that part of the continent. The same Frere gave a public speech in Glasgow three years later during which he outlined a scheme for the complete carving up of Africa among the European powers, not greatly unlike the one which was to take place in reality over the next quarter-century. Certainly in this he was a long way ahead of other publicists or politicians of the time – the Glasgow newspapers the following day almost unanimously ridiculed Frere's perspectives. Appointed Governor of Cape Colony and British High Commissioner in South Africa in 1877 he antagonised the Boers and provoked wars with the Xhosa and Zulus in pursuit of an endeavour to unite South Africa under British control. Clearly he was a portent of things to come.

Simultaneously, explorers, financed by geographical or religious societies, recounted their adventures in the British media, their eyes dazzled by spectacular natural phenomena, their mouths full of tales of untold wealth and commercial potential – not to mention millions of souls waiting to be gathered to Christ. David Livingstone, whose renown spread among the public in the early 1870s, was one such, undoubtedly replete with good intentions; the figure with whom his name is inseparably linked, the odious H. M. Stanley, had the commercial potential of his exploratory activities more firmly in view. The 1870s saw a quickening of commercial activity in Africa as elsewhere throughout the empire, but it must be emphasised that in that decade Africa, so far as British capital, government and public were concerned, remained as yet a relatively peripheral matter.

Political Forces

The swelling notes of the imperial theme beginning to sound in late Victorian Britain and soon to overwhelm every other political melody, were, for all Bartle Frere's percipience, orchestrated at this stage of development not so much in counting houses or stock exchanges, or for that matter in Whitehall offices, as in constituency associations and elite political clubs. A lot of significance is usually attached to the Crystal Palace speech made by the Conservative leader Disraeli in 1872, and its importance was certainly far-reaching. It was not, however, a call for the extension of imperial boundaries, but for a strengthened appreciation of the then existing empire as a unitary reality of world-historic significance presided over by the British crown and bathing the meanest voter of the country's electorate in its reflected glory.

It was in short a public relations or propagandist tactic. The Second Reform Act of 1867 and the Ballot Act of 1872 had created an enlarged electorate, embracing the more skilled and prosperous sections of the manual workforce, out of reach of traditional forms of electoral manipulation and influence. The bloc of wealth, privilege and political ascendancy with its foundations in landownership was menaced economically by shifts in world trade patterns and increasing agricultural competition and politically by the new constitutional structures. Even since 1832 it had faced a growing necessity, through its political embodiment, the Tory Party, to master the arts of mass politics, and in this it had been only indifferently successful. Following 1867 the need had become doubly urgent: the Liberal Party in 1868 decisively won the first election fought on the enlarged franchise and seemed likely to retain permanently the loyalty of the new electorate, threatening with permanent subordination a Conservative interest which up to that point had won outright only one election in twenty years.

To be sure, the rival Liberal bloc did not threaten the institutions of property or hierarchy in any dramatic fashion,[19] also it possessed its own very powerful landowning component and its own authoritarian religiosity. Nonetheless, if the Conservative Party was to survive as a major political actor it was compelled to effect a social mobilisation at a popular level such as it had never previously accomplished. Imperial rhetoric – though the outcome could not have been initially foreseen – proved to be the master key that unlocked countless doors.

Fighting for his party's life, Disraeli combined into a coherent ideological attack three of what would nowadays be termed 'discourses'. One form of appeal was straightforward and material: the Conservative Party was presented as the traditional if paternalist friend of the working man and the other victims of market society, the agent of paternalist *noblesse oblige* social reform in contrast to the heartless *laissez-faire* principles of Liberal nonconformism. A practical outcome was the deliberate courting of the trade union vote with a far more accommodating attitude to these organisations than Gladstone's administration had ever displayed.[20] Secondly and connectedly, an anti-puritanical nostalgia was invoked, with Conservatives portrayed as the hearty aristocratic defenders of popular lifestyles and pleasures that the nonconformist conscience which dominated the Liberal Party wanted to restrict or abolish – above all alcohol. The first of these three, though it may have helped the Conservatives to win the 1874 general election, had little impact in the long run. The second was a lot more potent and contributed significantly to the establishment of a bedrock of Conservative influence among the working population.

It was the third, however, which returned incomparable dividends. By channelling traditions of patriotic superiority with the distinct racist overtones lurking in the public consciousness, and combining them with the posture of aggressive truculence towards foreigners, especially 'uncivilised' ones, upon which earlier in the century Palmerston had founded his career, the 'imperial turn' inaugurated by Disraeli tapped into reserves of self-congratulatory sentiment transcending class boundaries and antagonistic class interests. It became increasingly as time went on the glue holding together the socially divergent Conservative bloc. The public school graduate seeking a vocation consistent with his background and training, the impoverished but aspiring white-collar clerk, the socially deferential workingman, could all worship at the shrine of the red-splashed world wall-map and feel themselves participants, whether leading or humble ones, in a mighty national destiny. It was not long before academic historians, and following them routine publicists and authors of school textbooks[21] were portraying the British empire as the providential culmination of superior moral and political virtue inherent in the Anglo-Saxon race, exhibited in a continuous line of development since the days of Alfred the Great.

If empire bound together a cross-class coalition it did no less for the economically and ideologically threatened central component of that bloc. If, with the irruption of mass politics, the hold of ancient elites on the British state itself was slipping, all the more could they find consolation in posturing as the high-profile rulers of a world-embracing empire. It was a departure moreover which lent itself naturally to the politics of spectacle, manufactured tradition and the ceremonial of power. A year after returning to office in 1874 Disraeli conferred upon Queen Victoria the title of Empress of India – a move which is said to have delighted the sovereign as much as it doubtless inspired feelings of pride and reverence in the Tory electorate. It was at the same time that the republican movement which had existed in England for several decades, sometimes attracting high-level adherents, was finally extinguished and the monarchy as an institution elevated into sacrosanct immunity from respectable public criticism.[22]

The latter development symbolised a still more profound shift in consciousness. The values associated with the 'New Imperialism', though a deliberate partisan construct of the Conservative Party in the early years of the 1870s, had caught a historic tide which made them in a remarkably short period the dominant values of society at large. Henceforth, the Liberals were in a dilemma they could never resolve. Compelled by the prevailing ideological winds to adopt the same values on their own account but unable wholeheartedly to do so, in relation to imperial issues they were perpetually on the defensive: it was the Conservatives who were enabled thereafter to wrap themselves in the imperial flag and present themselves as the most resolute defenders of all that was associated with it.

By the end of the 1870s Gladstone was in power again and, it must once more be stressed, the additions to imperial territory which had occurred in that decade were minimal still. Nonetheless, a process had been set in motion and acquired a historic momentum that would not be diverted by anything so minor as a change in government. The state was on the point of being driven irresistibly into the acquisition of a 'Third Empire'.

Further Reading

Paul Adelman, *Gladstone, Disraeli and Later Victorian Politics*, Longman, 1970. The political background.

P.J. Cain and A.G. Hopkins, *British Imperialism: Innovation and Expansion 1688–1914*, Longman, 1993. Exhaustive description and analysis, interpreting the growth of empire as being driven by 'gentlemanly capitalism'.

David Cannadine, 'The Empire Strikes Back', *Past & Present* 147, May 1995. Critique of Cain and Hopkins.

C.C. Eldridge, *Victorian Imperialism*, Hodder & Stoughton, 1978.

John Gallagher and Ronald Robinson, 'The Imperialism of Free Trade', *Economic History Review* 6, 1953. A seminal interpretation.

Freda Harcourt, 'Disraeli's Imperialism, 1866–1868: A Question of Timing', *Historical Journal* 23, 1980. Considers political motives.

Peter Mathias, *The First Industrial Nation*, Methuen, 1969. Wide-ranging and readable study of British economic development from the Industrial Revolution to 1914.

Andrew Porter, *European Imperialism 1870–1914*, Macmillan, 1994. Concise and very informative.

A.N. Porter, *An Atlas of British Overseas Expansion*, Routledge, 1991. Supplies the visual aids.

A.J. Stockwell (ed.), *Cambridge Illustrated History of the British Empire*, Cambridge University Press, 1996. Informative and analytical. Not to be mistaken for a coffee-table publication.

2
The Drive into Africa

The image of late nineteenth-century imperialism, both British and European generally, is associated inseparably with the African continent. Until the 1870s this great landmass had featured in the calculations of European business or European chancelleries only in particular aspects and at very specific individual points – although, certainly, some of these particularities were very important ones.

Geographic and climatic features were partly responsible for the general indifference – neither desert nor rainforest attracted a numerous European presence. More important, however, was the fact that these features, combined with distance, geographic obstacles and the existing forms of economic activity practised by African populations provided, once the slave trade was outlawed, only limited scope for drawing off an economic surplus whether by coercion or exchange, and one not likely to repay the costs of bases and transport in the interior of the continent. Were large-scale commercial penetration to take place the most likely route for it to follow was via Africa's three principal rivers, the Nile, the Niger and the Congo, but of these only the first was fully navigable, and that only at certain seasons.

The North African coast with its immediate hinterland formed a distinctive space set apart from the remainder of the continent. Long before the concept of Europe had been thought of it was part of an integrated Mediterranean economy and culture. The Islamic Arab invasions of the seventh century turned a highway into a frontier and ruptured the Mediterranean unity. Subsequently, the Arab empire centred in Baghdad had been superseded by a Turkish one ruled from Constantinople. By the early nineteenth century, with the political decay of this regime far advanced, the governors of its North African provinces were maintaining only a formal allegiance and behaving with perfect autonomy.[1] A major gap had also appeared in the empire's North African integrity, for one of these provinces, namely Algeria, had been seized by the French state in 1830 as an agricultural colony. In 1870 this was, apart from the British- and Dutch-descended polities in the far south, the only considerable European presence in the whole continent.

That latter presence, however, represented only part of the lively interest which Great Britain, as an imperial and world-dominant commercial power held in certain parts of the African coastline – one of the particularities referred to above. The security of communications both with its Indian empire, its Australasian colonies and the Far East generally were matters of critical importance. The colony at the Cape, whatever additional purposes it might serve, was primarily important because it controlled the long sea-route to the Indian Ocean. The short route, part of which was necessarily overland, ran through the middle eastern territories of the Turkish empire; consequently the stability, continuance and subservience of that state had become cardinal principles of British strategy and diplomacy. As Hobsbawm puts it: 'To preserve as much as possible of its privileged access to the non-European world was a matter of life and death for the British economy.'[2] The point was that this world was, during the last quarter of the century, undergoing the process of increasing European penetration.

Egypt

In 1869 the short land-route became a sea-route as well with the inauguration in that year of the Suez Canal, making Egypt an even more central concern than it already was. In 1870, 486 ships passed through it. Their total capacity was 436,000 tons, and 66 per cent of that was British. By 1910 the total tonnage amounted to 16.5 million, with 63 per cent of that being British. The canal had in fact been constructed with French capital, but, open to the shipping of all nations in the free-trade era that the world was assumed to be moving into, that was not seen in Whitehall as a problem – an indirect diplomatic paramountcy over Egypt's rulers was imagined to be all that would be necessary to preserve stability and the unrestricted development of commerce.

The Egyptian monarch, styled the Khedive, was formally subject to the suzerainty of the Turkish sultan, but to all intents and purposes exercised an independent power, which he used to authorise the canal and was rewarded for his compliance with a block of shares in the enterprise. The Egyptian regime of the time reproduced on a smaller stage that of its Turkish overlord, effectively a military despotism which used coercive power to extract a surplus out of the basic agricultural producers and attempted to push its rapacious hegemony southward up the Nile, bringing the populations of these regions into its taxation orbit. In the international commodity markets cotton produced in the Nile valley had come to assume a growing importance, especially following the disruptions of the American Civil War, and the newly opened canal promised to be a source of nearly limitless revenues.

The explosive combination of an archaic and decrepit semi-feudal state structure with the influx of western capital, technology and financiers soon resulted in bankruptcy for the monarch. The leading European powers responded in the manner to which they had become accustomed with states such as those of Turkey or the South American republics. Viable assets were bought out, in this case the Khedive's Suez Canal shares, which Disraeli, in a diplomatic coup, purchased on behalf of the British government. European financial experts were imposed upon the monarch by a consortium of the great powers to administer the Egyptian revenues and extract the debt payments; the peasantry 'now had the dubious benefits of western efficiency in tax gathering'.[3]

The toilers on the land were not in a position to do much about their grievances, but discontent crystalised in the peasant-based Egyptian army, destablising the regime of informal European direction. Following several years of political turmoil and insurrection, the British seized control of the country in 1882 following the naval bombardment of Alexandria, invasion of the country and defeat of the rebel Egyptian army.[4] On paper Egypt remained a Turkish province, with an international machinery of debt collection, but was in actuality run by the British consul-general, Evelyn Baring (later Lord Cromer). These developments were the responsibility not of the overt imperialist Disraeli, but of his ostensibly anti-imperialist rival Gladstone, who covered them with a variety of implausible and unconvincing justifications. In fact we know from the official record that the Liberal government dithered and wittered over what course of action to take: the outcome was nevertheless entirely satisfactory to the bondholders and the financial interests involved, amply demonstrating their capacity to shape the agenda even of supposedly unsympathetic administrations.[5]

General Gordon and the Sudan

For the meantime, following these upheavals, the British made the Khedive stop his attempts to extend his power southward, and the upper part of the Nile, the Sudan, was abandoned to Muslim fundamentalists who in 1883 successfully revolted against Egyptian overlordship. Even this withdrawal, however, had a significance in the annals of British imperialism, for it was tied in with the death in 1885 of the egregious General Gordon – who had delayed in Khartoum while exceeding his commission to organise the evacuation of Sudanese Christians – at the hands of these same Sudanese dervishes. His demise was turned into a resounding media event in Britain by a press, pulpit and music-hall lurching increasingly towards the right and the imperial idea.[6]

According to *The Times*

> The anxiety as to General Gordon's safety is not confined to London, or fomented by Opposition prints, as is sometimes suggested; it is discernible in the organs of all classes, those of the working men not excepted, and is plainly manifested in the North of England and Scotland, the strongholds of Liberalism.[7]

Once news of Gordon's death had reached Britain a day of national mourning was proclaimed.

The incident did much to undermine Gladstone and his administration, who were accused of 'betrayal and desertion' according to a leading churchman, and brought sinister consequences too for domestic and especially Irish policy, since its effect was to reinforce imperial intransigence and unwillingness to compromise with supposedly inferior cultures. So far as Africa was concerned, it became in due course an article of faith in Westminster that the headwaters of the river in the hands of any rival European power would constitute an intolerable menace to the irrigation of the entire Nile valley. Thus in the late 1890s, with imperial frenzy in both official and popular circles rising to its peak, the reconquest of the Sudan was deemed essential in view of a French expeditionary probe in that direction from their colonies to the southwest. General Kitchener was accordingly dispatched to annihilate the dervish power along with tens of thousands of dervishes and compel Colonel Marchand to remove the French flag from a vital British interest which no British eye had hitherto surveyed.

As noted, a clutch of European powers, great and small, were contemporaneously in the process of ravaging the continent and its populations. A look at the map demonstrates that in the main the British possessions tended, with some exceptions, to lie along a north–south axis between Cape Town and Egypt, and those of France, the second major plunderer, in a block from west to east – their intersection in 1898 brought the two powers into the confrontation on the Upper Nile. Around the edges were the prizes won by Germany, Portugal and Italy, and in the middle the enormous and enormously wealthy personal fief of the Belgian king, Leopold II.

We have already noted the reluctance of Gladstone's government in 1882 to undertake the invasion and virtual annexation of Egypt which it eventually carried through. Rather surprisingly, and apparently in contradiction to the developing ideology of frenetic imperialism in the rival party, the same attitudes tended to characterise the mostly Conservative administrations of the high imperialist era.[8] It has to be remembered that the ruling class was never a unified entity, and that even its principal sectors – political, financial, administrative, landowning industrial, military – much as they overlapped, were at the same time within themselves fragmented and divided. For those with direct government responsibility imperial excursions sponsored directly by the state meant expenditure (it might even mean additional taxation), questions in the House, debates and the possibility – as Gladstone discovered with Gordon – of acute embarrassment if things went badly wrong.

Chartered Companies

It was therefore considered to be enormously preferable to have imperial excursions undertaken indirectly and if possible at private expense – one is almost tempted to describe them as private finance initiatives. To this end British governments in the 1880s revived an institution enormously important in the earlier phases of imperialism, but which had since the 1850s and the Indian revolt against the rule of the East India Company fallen into discredit: namely the chartered company. These were in essence commercial organisations equipped by the British state with governmental powers, including those of waging war and levying taxes. In respect of the African partition three were established, the initiative in demanding chartered status being taken by their proprietors, who regarded delegated sovereignty as a necessary adjunct to their commercial operations if they were to be enabled to realise the fabulous economic potential they envisaged in the African interior. They were respectively in dates of establishment, the Royal Niger Company (RNC), the Imperial British East Africa Company, and the British South Africa Company (BSAC).

East Africa

Of the three, the second of these, Ibea (as it was customarily entitled), was the least substantial although its actions were still decisive for the immediate and long-term future of millions of Africans. Founded by William Mackinnon, a Scottish shipowner with India-based interests, it was formed to exploit perceived golden opportunities inland from Zanzibar and acquired its charter in 1888. In commercial terms, however, its progress belied its promise, due partly to Mackinnon's lack of competence and partly to the company's failure to exact subsidies for a railway link from an economy-conscious government. However, it did succeed in imposing its overlordship upon the African kingdoms to the south of Lake Victoria and eastward to the Sultan of Zanzibar's coastal territory – which was the *quid pro quo* that Whitehall expected for the charter, a British presence in that area on account of the official sensitivities about the Upper Nile, whose source lay in that region.

Meantime in 1890 a formal protectorate was declared over Zanzibar and the coastline,[9] which since Bartle Frere's treaty of 1872 with the sultan the British had regarded as lying within their sphere. However, by the later 1880s commercial potential was evident and also the Germans were starting to show an interest.[10] The combination of state power and private finance was intended to be an economical solution, with the government taking responsibility for the smaller and more easily controlled area and the company for the geographically much more difficult regions of East Africa.

This arrangement began to unravel, however, with Ibea's bankruptcy and threat to evacuate its newly acquired dominions. In response Westminster and Whitehall showed a willingness to leave East Africa to its own devices in the meantime, confident that the region had been diplomatically insulated from rival predators. When the intention was made public, however, the short-lived Liberal government (1892–95) was assailed by an orchestrated campaign on the part of churches, press and chambers of commerce, which compelled it to change course and erect protectorates over what became Uganda and inland Kenya. The lobbying groups argued on the one hand that important commercial opportunities would be lost if the Lakes region fell under the control of a protectionist power, and on the other that Christian converts would be put in danger if removed from European protection and the missionary work of the churches undone.

How important the latter could be was demonstrated much further south, in the region around Lake Nyassa, to the south of German East Africa and west of Mozambique. The initiative in this case had been taken by missionaries of the Church of Scotland and the Free Church of Scotland, who had not confined themselves to preaching the gospel and philanthropic activity in the tradition of Livingstone, but had assumed governing powers over the Africans, not excluding capital punishment. No British administration, in the circumstances and the public feeling of the time, could possibly allow a territory in such a delicate condition to fall under foreign control, and accordingly when the despised Portuguese threatened to annex it the area was taken under British protection in 1891 as the Central African Protectorate, later Nyasaland, now Malawi.

South and Central Africa

Twelve years after the Egyptian occupation, a long chain of territories either claimed formally by Britain or reserved for subsequent occupation stretched southward through the Rift valley and beyond, while from the south another thrust, if anything even more unashamedly brutal and rapacious, advanced to meet them. This too was the achievement of a chartered company. In South Africa the formal British colonies of Cape Colony and Natal had coexisted uneasily since the earlier part of the century with the semi-independent Boer republics of the Orange Free State and the Transvaal (or South African Republic), all of them founded upon the subjugation and reduction to servile agricultural labour of the black population, though a certain minimum of African civic rights was preserved in Cape Colony.[11]

In the 1860s, however, the world's biggest concentration of diamonds and in the 1880s of gold were found within the borders of the republics, transforming white relations with the Africans, whose male population now came into demand as cheap mining labour, and Boer relations with the British, whose capital flooded in to exploit the opportunities, along with the workforce,[12] and whose governments now viewed the internal politics of the South African eldorado as a crucial imperial concern. Large numbers of non-Afrikaans whites, the 'Uitlanders' also entered the republics to take advantage of the demand for skilled labour which the mines generated, but were denied citizenship by a government determined not to allow its local culture to be swamped by these immigrants. The tangle of political, commercial and ideological contradictions which these developments generated were embodied in the person of Cecil Rhodes, a megalomaniac adventurer who made himself a millionaire by speculation in the diamond trade, and backed by his enormous wealth entered Cape Colony politics.

A mystic racist, stuffed with fantasies about the historic destiny of the Anglo-Saxon stock and possessed with visions of an all-British hegemony from 'the Cape to Cairo',[13] Rhodes played upon London's growing concerns about possible ambitions for full independence and territorial expansion on the part of the Transvaal, possibly in collaboration with the Portuguese or Germans, and by such means in 1889 secured a charter for his own British South Africa Company[14] to appropriate the strategically important central African territories to the north (which might in addition contain equally fabulous concentrations of mineral wealth) before any of the rivals could stake a claim.

Equipped with these advantages and the premiership of Cape Colony, Rhodes recruited a gang of mercenaries and desperadoes and by-passing the Transvaal dispatched them on a land-seizing expedition in the style of Spanish conquistadores. The 'treaty' concluded with the most powerful of the African rulers in the area is sufficiently illustrative of their methods:

> Know all men by these presents that whereas Charles Dunnell Rudd of Kimberly, Rochfort Maguire of London, and Francis Robert Thompson of Kimberly ... the grantees, have covenanted and agreed ... to pay to me, my heirs and successors the sum of one hundred pounds sterling British currency on the first day of every lunar month and further to deliver to my Royal Kraal one thousand Martini-Henry breech-loading rifles, together with one hundred thousand rounds of suitable ball cartridges ... and further to deliver on the Zambesi River a steamboat with guns suitable for defensive purposes ... I Lo Bengula, King of the Matabele ... in the exercise of my sovereign powers ... do hereby grant and assign unto the said grantees ... the complete and exclusive charge over all metals and minerals situated and contained in my kingdom ... and to grant no concessions of land or mining rights from and after this date without their consent and concurrence.[15]

When Lobenguela understood the claims he was supposed to have conceded he tried to denounce the treaty, so Rhodes's agents proceeded from the force of diplomacy to the diplomacy of force. African resistance was soon subdued, their land and cattle plundered and company rule imposed in the new territories, which Rhodes naturally had named after himself. The Cape-to-Cairo project was thereby realised, apart from a single gap created by the existence of German East Africa (Tanganyika).

Nigeria

In another part of the continent, British colonial possessions were clustered in separate sections along the coastal bulge of West Africa, all of them expanded from the stations which were nearly abandoned in the 1860s. The construction of the largest, Nigeria, was also intimately associated with the appearance of a chartered company. The great river had been in the eighteenth century a highway for the conveyance of human cargoes to the slave ships waiting for them at the coast, and in its enormous delta African monarchs who thrived as middlemen in the business had established a group of small but wealthy kingdoms or 'city states'. With the abandonment of the human commerce the former British slavers, mostly based on Liverpool, and the delta rulers with whom they were linked, had diversified into vegetable and palm oil, which, as the principal basis for soap manufacture in Britain, found a ready market.

Local trade wars, both metaphorical and literal, erupted in the delta when a Glasgow firm tried with some success to compete with the Liverpool cartel and expand the area of the trade up the river to the extent that it was navigable. In a fashion increasingly characteristic of the late nineteenth century the dispute was settled by amalgamation. The resulting conglomerate, the National African Company under Sir George Goldie, an opportunist merchant, was accorded chartered status and a government-backed trade monopoly in 1886 as the Royal Niger Company. As with eastern, southern and central Africa the motive was to retain – on the cheap – as large a region as possible within the sphere of British economic and political hegemony, a purpose that fitted admirably with the commercial aims of the local interests and their backers.

The company was authorised to

carry on business and to act as merchants, bankers, traders, commission agents, ship-owners, carriers, or in any other capacity in the United Kingdom, Africa or elsewhere. And to import, export, buy, sell, barter, exchange, pledge, make advances upon or otherwise deal in goods, produce, articles and merchandize ...

To form or acquire and carry on trading stations, factories, stores, and depots in Africa or elsewhere ...

... and whereas ... the Kings, Chiefs, and other peoples of various territories in the basin of the River Niger ... have ceded the whole of their respective territories to the Company ... and whereas the Company ... have purchased the business of all the European traders in the region aforesaid and are now the sole European traders ...

... to hold and retain the full benefit of the several cessions aforesaid or any of them, and all rights, interests, authorities, and powers for the purposes of government, preservation of public order, protection of the said territories, or otherwise of what nature or kind soever.[16]

The charter went on to prohibit the RNC from establishing a trade monopoly, or discriminating commercially against foreign nationals, but effectively negated the significance of that prohibition by stipulating that 'foreigners alike with British subjects will be subject to administrative dispositions in the interests of commerce and order'.

The Company exacted over 350 treaties from potentates in the northern part of what was to become Nigeria (the British government having
already established a protectorate over what was then known as the Oil
Rivers – the Niger delta). Its agents carried with them sheaves of blank
treaty forms, which varied marginally according to circumstances, but
typically took the following form:

> Treaty made on the   day of,   18,   between the Chiefs of on the one
> hand, and the Royal Niger Company (Chartered and Limited) ...
> 1. We, the undersigned Chiefs of, with the consent of our people, and
> with the view of bettering their condition, do on this day cede to the
> Company, and their assigns, for ever, the whole of our territory; but the
> Company shall pay private owners a reasonable amount for any por-
> tion of land that the Company may require from time to time.[17]
> 2. We hereby give to the Company and their assigns, for ever, full juris-
> diction of every kind; and we pledge ourselves not to enter into any
> war with other tribes without the sanction of the Company.
> 3. We also give to the Company and their assigns, for ever, the sole right
> to mine in our territory ...
>   ... we hereby approve, and accept it for ourselves and our people with
> their consent, and in testimony of this, having no knowledge of writ-
> ing,[18] do affix our marks below it, and I,   , for and on behalf of the
> Company, do hereby affix my hand ...

It can be acknowledged that compared to the 'treaty' (known as the Rudd
Concession) by which Rhodes's agent established the BSAC claim to
Matebeleland the RNC counterpart appears almost as a model of legal re-
straint and responsibility

The RNC went on to acquire, by such diplomacy or by force when necessary, the northern half of the future Nigeria, bringing into its orbit an
enormous territory incorporating the utmost diversity of ethnic group-
ings, religions and cultures. The government in London was well satis-
fied, for it had the objective in mind of preventing the French from gain-
ing any colonial foothold on the navigable stretch of the lower Niger, and
this the Company successfully accomplished. In 1899 the RNC had its
charter withdrawn, but by then it hardly mattered, for the government,
prodded by the arch-imperialist Joseph Chamberlain, assumed responsibility for maintaining political control and the company was entrenched
in the commercially dominant position from which it went on to form a
central component in the Unilever commercial empire of the twentieth
century.

The institution of the three chartered companies between 1886 and 1889 reflected the fact that by the middle of the decade Africa had assumed the position of a zone of contention for territory and influence among the powers of western Europe and marked a novel stage of the coalescence of governmental power with the projects of particular commercial organisations. The resulting competition, confrontation and shifting alliances between the participating states during the 1880s and 1890s foreshadowed and rehearsed their greater and more strongly directed appetites during the first decade of the twentieth century, as well as the tightening of military partnerships which were only resolved in the end with the outbreak of a general European war.[19]

Imperial Rivalries

However, that was for later. Armed hostilities between the rival colonisers threatened from time to time in the course of the African scramble but never actually broke out. On the face of it the explanation might appear to be that the consolidated blocs which ultimately went to war were yet to fully develop the political and military tendencies which led to that outcome. In the 1880s these were still embryonic. While it is true that what was only a potential in 1884 had thirty years later developed into a certainty, the reasons for the avoidance of European war over Africa was not so much because the pressures pushing towards it were less than they were in Europe in 1914, but because the stakes and the risks were always high and reached far beyond Africa while none of Great Britain's rivals found it worthwhile to challenge it where vital interests were at stake.

The nature of capitalism as a world system in the 1880s, within a framework of nation states evolved in an earlier phase of social development, already pointed towards the likelihood of a generalised conflict at some point in the future to settle the question of global ascendancy. Each participant was even by that time well down the road (despite immediate world recession) in the expansion of its industrial potential and new technologies, with massive investment in improved firepower. The diplomatic/military quadrille had already begun, but Africa was never a suitable theatre in which to initiate the conflict.

The global stakes were far too important to endanger for any particular economic gain or favourable media publicity in a faraway African (or Asiatic) outpost. In practice, whenever a dispute of such a kind appeared, after a space of diplomatic posturing and bellicose publicity the power that was locally weakest on the ground conceded the claim. Since Britain, thanks to its position on the Nile and the Niger and on the southern edge of the continent, not to speak of its world-beating navy, was invariably the strongest player, it naturally won the confrontations it regarded as really important, though sometimes conceding claims whenever a useful trade-off might be achieved.

The Berlin Conference

The fact that by the mid-1880s the race to dismember Africa was obviously in train led among the powers to the search for rules by which it might be regulated, ones designed to minimise so far as possible the dangers of an unforeseen explosion resulting from actions on the part of their agents over which the home governments had no immediate control. In 1885 the West African Conference met in Berlin – including representatives from the USA – to specify ground rules for annexation and takeover. The title was misleading, for the scope of the discussions and line-rulings on the map covered the whole of the continent.

The conference had to deal with the ownership of Africa. It did not specify to whom every square kilometre was to belong – although certainly it was assumed that none of it belonged to the Africans – but allocated some slices that were the subject of immediate covetousness, and for the remainder stipulated what was to count for recognition as effective occupation in the future. Among the former arrangements the principal decision was to settle the future of the Congo river and its basin.

This gigantic waterway drained most of the rainforest area of central Africa but was rendered unnavigable to the sea by precipitous falls and rapids only a few kilometres from its mouth. But for this geographical accident there can be little doubt that European penetration, regardless of the very unfavourable climate, would have been extended far upriver at a much earlier stage. The Portuguese indeed were already entrenched on the short navigable stretch. No European had any idea of what the economic potential of the rainforest might turn out to be, but hopes were high: preliminary probes by small expeditions showed that it abounded in at least two commodities in high contemporary demand – ivory and wild rubber.

British interests were attracted but, unlike the other two great continental rivers, no close connection of a historic or contemporary nature could be plausibly advanced. The costs and difficulties of direct British occupation and control were unthinkable, but cabinets, whether Liberal or Conservative, took it for granted that it was worth making very considerable efforts to ensure an open door for British commerce and speculation in this land of tropical promise. It was hoped at first that the aim could be attained through an arrangement with the weak power already *in situ*, the Portuguese, albeit this state was notoriously protectionist, but strenuous objections were voiced by British commercial interests acting through the Chambers of Commerce of big cities, especially Manchester. French and German interests objected no less strenuously, and the British government could not afford to alienate both its own merchants and two major foreign powers – hence the conference.

In the event, since the main powers could not acceptably compose their mutual suspicions and rivalries, the river basin and much more beside was handed over to the royal entrepreneur who since the 1870s, had been energetically lobbying the various governments for the concession with public propaganda and behind-the-scenes intrigue, and who had sent H. M. Stanley with an armed force to the river to give material backing to his claims. For the British, French and German governments it represented a more than adequate compromise, relieving them of the expense and re-sponsibility of opening up, policing and defending this enormous entity but with – they thought – an open door and the continuing hope of pick-ing up the pieces if King Leopold's initially rickety Congo Free State were to collapse. Portuguese objections could be discounted: it was a minor power. Moreover, the Belgian monarch had made solemn promises to maintain a regime of free trade and religious and humanitarian endeav-our – undertakings which he broke at once to seize exclusive commercial access and install a colonial machine of unabashed criminality, grisly even by the accepted imperial standards.

The Boer Republics

European inter-state disputes over Africa in the subsequent fifteen years were not always so smoothly and amicably resolved as at Berlin, but they were never allowed to escalate to the level of having to be settled by mili-tary force. The one occasion when a European power did have to commit serious human and monetary resources was of a different sort, though not without its overtones of international threat. The existence of the Boer republics, whose culturally offensive rulers grew more intransigent the more mineral royalties enhanced their state income, represented an anomaly from the point of view of British capital and British power, the more so as German finance, with cheap loans and sympathy, tried to use them as an entry point to the fabulous riches of the Rand.

Various schemes were employed to ensure their due subservience. Brit-ain claimed a vaguely defined paramountcy and control over their exter-nal affairs. They were shut off from expansion westward, northward or from the acquisition of a coastline. In 1895 Cecil Rhodes sponsored a private-enterprise *coup d'état* to overthrow the Transvaal government and install a more accommodating one. Its spectacular failure left full-scale warfare as the only remaining recourse, which duly broke out four years later. In a number of ways the South African War (1899–1902) marked the climax of British imperialism in view both of its scale – the Boers resisted effectively and were subdued with great difficulty – and of its objectives, which were nothing less than to bring the incalculably valuable goldfields, central to the stability of world finance, and their labour force under an acceptable British-aligned regime. At the same time, the war and eventual victory, although it aroused temporary ecstasies of rejoicing among the British public, stimulated considerable opposition as well, and almost universally unfavourable foreign reaction to British conquest of the republics revealed the degree of international isolation into which the state had drifted and the urgent necessity of mended fences and tighter diplomatic–military ties with one or other of the two European military blocs in the process of formation.

Official Attitudes

Looking in broad measure from a British perspective at the conquests, annexations and quasi-annexations in Africa between the 1870s and the end of the century, the central reality for all involved was that ultimately only the government could make legally binding treaties, offer long-term protection, wage prolonged war or claim international recognition – although as we have noted, some of these powers could be leased out. Anyone, therefore, who was anxious for any of these things to happen had to bring Downing Street and Westminster into the equation, either in a direct role or as a source of delegated authority. It is remarkable that with a few minor exceptions they nearly always succeeded in doing so. Prime ministers, foreign secretaries and cabinets, who had their own, and in their own eyes usually more important, business to attend to were well aware that as the continent was increasingly brought within the circuits of international capital movements, Britain could not afford to be left out of the bargaining. Generally, the administrations would have preferred to attain their objectives without assuming direct responsibility, but equally in most cases that option was not long available. As Victor Kiernan puts it:

> Wavering between objective and subjective – between what ministers were really doing or allowing to be done, and what they liked to think or wanted others to think, they were doing – grows more pronounced.

Conquest of the Sudan and the Transvaal 'at first sight ... might suggest a full-blooded drive for empire': but ... 'this was not how ministers saw their onslaughts'. Finally we see another old premier, sick and sorry, brought face to face with realization that the jingo party had rigged things in such a way that he and Britain *must* go to war – 'and all for people who we despise, and for territory which will bring no profit and no power to England'. In other words Lord Salisbury simply did not know why the Boer War was about to be fought.[20]

By the time the Boers capitulated all major objectives in Africa were apparently achieved, but the realisation was beginning to dawn, even among some of the most convinced and obsessive imperialists, that the problems of consolidating that success into a permanent and tightly knit asset were only beginning.

Further Reading

P.J. Cain and A.G. Hopkins, *British Imperialism: Innovation and Expansion 1688–1914*; Longman, 1993.

M.E. Chamberlain, *The Scramble for Africa*, Longman, 1974.

C.C. Eldridge, *Victorian Imperialism*, Hodder & Stoughton, 1978.

John E. Flint, *Sir George Goldie and the Making of Nigeria*, Oxford University Press, 1960.

J.S. Galbraith, *Crown and Charter: The Early Years of the British South Africa Company*, University of California Press, 1974.

J.S. Galbraith, *Mackinnon and East Africa 1878–1895*, Cambridge University Press, 1972.

L.H. Gann and Peter Duigan, *The Rulers of British Africa 1870–1914*, Croom Helm, 1978. Written from a pro-imperial standpoint.

W.G. Hynes, *The Economics of Empire: Britain, Africa and the New Imperialism 1870–1895*, Longman, 1975.

V.G. Kiernan, *The Lords of Human Kind*, Weidenfeld & Nicolson, 1969. Discusses imperial attitudes.

J.M. MacKenzie, *The Partition of Africa*, Methuen, 1983. Brief but informative.

J. Forbes Munro, *Britain in Tropical Africa 1880–1960*, Macmillan, 1984. Concise and useful.

Ronald Olivier and G.N. Sanderson (eds), *The Cambridge History of Africa*, Vol. 6, c. *1870–1905*, Cambridge University Press, 1985.

R. Robinson and J. Gallagher, *Africa and the Victorians*, Macmillan, 1961. The classic 'revisionist' interpretation, downplaying economic considerations.

3
Other Extensions

If the partition of Africa was the most spectacular theatre of imperial expansion in the late nineteenth century, it was far from being the only one. From any rational perspective the Pacific and Indian oceans were of far greater importance than Africa to the imperial powers, even if the developments taking place in the eastern hemisphere at that time were on the whole less noisy and colourful.

India

According to Cain and Hopkins, 'the full value of British rule, the return on political investments first made in the eighteenth century, was not realised until the second half of the nineteenth century, when India became a vital market for Lancashire's cotton goods and when other specialised interests, such as jute manufacturers in Dundee and steel producers in Sheffield also increased their stake in the sub-continent'.[1] The importance to the cotton textile industry can be measured by the anxiety with which Lancashire merchants, led by the Manchester Chamber of Commerce, scrutinised the endeavours made by the Indian government to levy revenue duties on cotton goods and the success with which they usually got them blocked or lowered – though in other respects their efforts to influence government action were much less successful.

Trade, however, was only one aspect of India's importance. It absorbed £286 million of the capital raised on the London stock market between 1865 and 1913, around 18 per cent of the empire's total, and second in importance to Canada for such investment.[2] India itself became a base for the further extension of the investment network, with the National Bank of India, founded in Calcutta in 1863, establishing offices in Ceylon, Burma and East Africa. Among its directors was Sir William Mackinnon, the same

individual whose Imperial British East Africa Company played a significant role, as noted in Chapter 2, in bringing about annexations in that
area. Not only that, he was a close friend of Bartle Frere – whose influence
we have encountered at several points already – and, as Cain and Hopkins
express it, 'cultivated connections' with civil servants in a position to further his interests. The successor to Mackinnon's commercial empire, James
Mackay, was so well connected that he only just failed to become Viceroy
of India.

However, important though commercial connections with India undoubtedly were, it was financial ones that were really central. Towards the
end of the century external debt burdens were so heavy that revenue from
taxation and exports could no longer cover them and payments could only
be balanced by borrowing. The debt to external creditors amounted to half
the value of the country's exports. One of the crucial advantages of free
trade was that it enabled surpluses earned by India from trade with Europe, Asia and the United States to be used to clear its deficit with the UK,
and 'this in turn was vital to the maintenance of the pattern of multilateral
settlements which enabled Britain, in turn, to settle more than two-fifths
of her own trading deficits'.[3] Since local Indian manufactures helped to
reduce imports and thus the deficit, the government in India actually
tended to favour them as against British exporters.

The exchange rate of the rupee against sterling also presented problems
of a highly complex nature. The eventual solution, reached towards the
end of the century, was, as Cain and Hopkins demonstrate, favourable to
financial and City interests and disappointing to British manufacturers,
particularly cotton producers. The essence of British relations with the
subcontinent is well summed up by these two authors: 'The twin impera-
tives of holding the Raj together and keeping faith with external creditors
exercised a pervasive, almost determining, effect on British policy in India.'[4] In short, the nature of the empire in India cannot be understood
merely with reference to what was happening in India itself, or even in
the sphere of Anglo-Indian relationships alone. It becomes comprehen-
sible only when the Indian empire is understood as a component in a global system. Cain and Hopkins normally avoid eloquent passages, but they
permit themselves one when stating their conclusion in relation to India:
'By perceiving these connections, we can improve our appreciation of the
value of the jewel in the crown and the reasons for keeping it polished
and protected.'[5]

East Asia

China

On the face of things the dealings of British government and British capital in China were far closer to a textbook illustration of the Leninist model of imperial relationships growing directly out of state-supported monopoly capitalism seeking cheap investment opportunities than anything that happened in Africa. Moreover, the rivalries of European powers – and of the USA – in China were of an explicit and wholly unmistakable economic character.

Since the seventeenth century European writers and observers had voiced astonishment at the size and sophistication of the Ch'ing empire, its mechanical ingenuity, despite the lack of the power sources employed in Europe, and the range of artefacts produced by its industrious and multitudinous populace. They had been no less impressed by its apparent social and political stability, attributed to the probity and philosophic understanding of its intensively literate and educated administrative class.

The prospects for trade relations appeared to be excellent, and indeed in the eighteenth century a very significant commerce developed, conducted through the East India Company, which acquired a legal monopoly of British trade. The Chinese commodities which supplied not only a British market, but, through British middlemen, a European one, were principally tea and silks. In the absence of any comparable Chinese demand for western products, the balance was at this stage cleared in silver.

Changing circumstances in the earlier part of the nineteenth century destabilised the structure. At the same time as a dynamic British economy, subject nonetheless to recurrent trade cycles and contracted markets, sought fresh commercial outlets, shortage of silver specie presented a growing and serious obstacle to the China trade, while in 1833 the East India Company lost its monopoly, thereby multiplying the number of would-be participants in Chinese commerce. A solution was discovered, however, in the shape of opium, produced in India and shipped to China,[6] which proved an effective substitute for silver. The Ch'ing state was by this time in an advanced state of political decay and weakening central authority, but, concerned at what the opium trade was doing to the public health of its subjects, tried to prohibit the transactions and was so disrespectful of property rights as to have stocks of the drug seized and destroyed. The response of the British, supported by other European powers and the USA, was to use its superior weaponry to compel the Chinese authorities to accommodate themselves to western notions of civilisation and opium consumption. By 1860, after the fighting was over, in two separated phases, a network of institutions had been put in place specifically designed to bring China irreversibly within the sphere of world exchange and the circuits of capital accumulation.

A British commercial base was established by the seizure, under the pretext of a lease, of Hong Kong. Around the coast treaty ports, with European rights of extra-territoriality, were designed to tap the presumed enormous interior trade, and they were intended to be 'bridgeheads to the interior, releasing the export potential of the hinterland and acting as funnels for a return trade in goods from Britain and India'.[7] The Son of Heaven was obliged to accept foreign officials stationed in his capital to exert direct pressure whenever required. Above all, to meet the heavy financial indemnities levied upon the Chinese government by the victors, control of customs collection in the Chinese ports was placed under the supervision of a British inspector-general.

A significant trade did develop in the treaty and other ports, but it had to be handled through Chinese middlemen, the 'comparador bourgeoisie', and came nowhere near to fulfilling the extravagant expectations associated with it. Trade with the interior remained obstinately underdeveloped, partly on account of institutional obstacles but to a much greater extent simply because of cultural resistance from the Chinese population to imported European manufactures. This disappointment, however, emphatically did not mean that commercial opportunities were absent in relation to China: other means existed of extracting a profit – 'as much in the management of the funds and exchanges as in any other way'.[8] The most renowned Far East expatriate firm, Jardine Matheson & Co., abandoned the opium trade in the 1870s to diversify into shipping, banking and trafficking in money rather than goods. More advanced still in this field was the Hong Kong and Shanghai Bank, which, as well as being a commercial enterprise, handled the funds both of the colonial government of the island and of the customs administration.

The Bank's great opportunity arrived when from the mid-1870s the Ch'ing rulers themselves began to contract foreign loans on the security of the customs income. On the first of these, the British Minister in Peking was a major subscriber, mixing business with diplomacy. For the remainder of the century, using its standing in the City of London and the interconnections noted above,[9] the bank floated most of these loans on Peking's behalf, particularly following the latter's defeat by the rising military imperialism of Japan in 1895 and imposition of another huge indemnity.[10] In view of such (scarcely voluntary) closer relations with the west, to which was added in 1900 the trauma of conjoint intervention by various powers to suppress the popular insurrection known as the Boxer Rising, the long-term passive resistance by Peking to European commercial penetration of the interior began to buckle.

Concessions for railway construction and mining operations (Cain and Hopkins refer to 'vast allocations') began to be handed out, particularly in the Yangtze valley, assumed to be the most promising area for opening up. Investment syndicates from all over Europe sprang up like mushrooms to exploit the new potential, with British ones very much in the forefront and those already well entrenched in a specially favourable position. Jardine Matheson combined with the Hong Kong and Shanghai Bank to set up the British and Chinese Corporation, which was additionally connected to Rothschilds and Barings in the City. Another British syndicate was linked to South African mining interests.

The closest relations existed between the most powerful of these consortia and the British Foreign Office, which backed with enthusiasm the operations of the Hong Kong and Shanghai Bank and underwrote loans to develop the new concessions. The bank's founder was for a time Chairman of the P & O shipping line and an MP from 1884 until 1900. The manager of the bank was effectively the author of a new treaty imposed by Britain on the Ch'ing following the eradication of the Boxers. It specified among other things a uniform currency and a national bank, with adoption of the gold standard as a long-term aim.

Only a modest measure of railway construction and no blossoming of European industrial enterprise in China followed in the wake of these treaties, loans and concessions, much to the annoyance of the Foreign Office. There is no mystery about the disappointing and apparently paradoxical outcome. European capital in general and British in particular was attracted to the prospect of high returns with minimal risk. That was to be found, it was hoped and expected, through trade in the products of China's indigenous handicraft industries and agricultural output, or better still in financial transactions, most attractively government borrowing, if the repayments could be made secure. Local antagonism to European practices, whatever the supine central government might decree, might make long-term investment in the deep interior very risky indeed, as the Boxers dramatically emphasised, but unlike the South American states or the Ottoman sultanate, the Ch'ing empire maintained its credit rating and was never in default. It is not to be wondered at therefore that British capital preferred as far as possible to stick to the coast where European power could be brought to bear or to seek safety in banking and handling safe government loans.

The capacity of the Ch'ing and its administrative apparatus to screw limitless resources out of its long-suffering population to service the debt was probably the central reason why the empire was never partitioned. There were certainly others. The stupefying expense and difficulty of actually controlling large tracts of Chinese territory were undoubtedly a major deterrent to the powers (though in the end it failed to deter Japanese imperialism). However, by the later years of the century the British, though maintaining their lead, no longer had the field almost exclusively to themselves: international competition was growing stronger. In the 1880s the French seized what Peking regarded as its own tropical provinces of Indo-China,[11] and a decade later not only Japan but France, Germany and Russia were chasing loans, concessions, influence and, in the case of Japan and Russia, manageable bits of peripheral territory.

From the British point of view, however, maintenance of the central authority was a far preferable option,[12] partly because the Europeans could bully it into enforcing order in the European interest for the benefit of traders, missionaries, concession hunters and collections of expatriate Europeans. The use of direct European power to suppress the Boxers was a unique undertaking; there could be no question of keeping a joint military presence on permanent duty to police the enormous country. Even more to the point, a functioning Ch'ing government was the best guarantee available that customs officers and tax collectors would continue to operate, that the debt repayments would continue to be met and that the large investment sunk into the loans over the years would be kept out of danger.[13]

Nevertheless, had the accelerating political decay at the centre after 1900 threatened to end with the breakup of the empire, an attempt would probably have been made, in spite of formidable risks and difficulties and as a last resort for 'maintaining order', to partition the country, probably through some form of international agreement that would accommodate the diverse interests and states clamouring to get themselves more favourably positioned at the trough. The actual course of events, however, demonstrates that there were good reasons why an imperialist policy might seek to *avoid* partition and find its interests – depending on whose these interests were – better served by the maintenance of semi-colony status rather than going the entire distance to annexation. Evidently, the long-established and well-entrenched British saw matters from a different perspective than the intrusive Japanese.

Feudal China was entering its final crisis, eroded by the same processes of historic decrepitude that had destroyed preceding dynasties and fatally undermined by the popular hatred that its subservience to foreign powers evoked among the people. Its end did not take the form of secession by provincial leaders but collapse at the centre. In 1911 revolution in the capital overthrew the monarchy, and 'overturned the regime supported by the foreign powers, raised the possibility of default on existing loans and opened up the prospect of a renewed scramble for China',[14] but since the revolutionaries looked towards western political and cultural models, the situation, from an imperialist standpoint, might yet be saved. The Foreign Office and the Hong Kong and Shanghai Bank moved quickly, to establish an International Commission of Bankers so as to avert uncontrollable foreign rivalries; to back Yuan Shih-K'ai, the political general most likely to preserve the financial status quo; and to advance the loan which enabled him to seize control of the government and suppress the democratic revolutionaries. They might have saved themselves the trouble. No long-term stability could hope to emerge from such manoeuvres and the country was to remain in a state of crisis-ridden disintegration for decades to come – but within three years European war was to transform the circumstances both of China and the world.

Japan

By contrast with the constant worries over the stability of the Chinese state and its threatened collapse from time to time, British financiers and British governments were more than gratified by the alacrity and commitment with which its Japanese counterpart adjusted to the realities of the global accumulation regime. The adoption of western models in economic and military affairs, administration and, to some degree, cultural practices such as diet and clothing, were happily funded with western loans. The Japanese experience was a model of what British imperialism would have liked to see occur on the mainland opposite – all the merchants and investors wanted was a stable regime with an open door for trade and, more importantly, lending. By the beginning of the twentieth century Japan was judged to be sufficiently civilised and militarily formidable to be accepted as Britain's formal ally – the first such specific commitment the British government had made since the rival European alliance systems began to form in the 1870s.

The consolidation of capitalist relations in southern Asia and around the eastern Pacific during the late nineteenth century was a general and multinational tendency and where suitable 'native' authorities could not be found capable of holding the framework together, occupation and annexation followed.[15] Since the seventeenth century the Dutch had claimed suzerainty over the greater part of the Indonesian archipelago, an invaluable producer of spices; but their effective occupation was for a long time limited, mostly to the island of Java and not even all of that. In the later nineteenth century the effective conquest of all the territories in their internationally acknowledged sphere of influence was seriously put in hand, constituting one of the less well-known bloody passages in establishing the era of European world hegemony.[16]

South East Asia

The British extended their hegemony in Burma and in North Borneo as well as in Malaya, the latter proving itself to be a metaphorical gold mine when it was discovered that its climate and soil were ideal for the cultivation of imported rubber plants, and that large deposits of tin were available for exploitation.[17] The Malayan peninsula did not, however, possess, unlike Siam or China, a unified monarchy which could be recruited as an imperial agent, and so the British, to establish control, had to deal with a host of minor potentates, who were placed in a position equivalent to that of the Indian princes under the British Raj. Formally Malaya, apart from the Straits Settlements, was not a colony but a series of protectorates (from 1896 the Federated Malay States). The local potentates were ruled by British 'advisers' who controlled revenue, land allocation, police, public works and medical services. The Governor of the Straits Settlements expressed the official view succinctly:

> I concur with Sir William Robinson in thinking that did we so abandon them their state would probably be worse than it was when we first intervened. I do not think that anything could justify us in leaving them to anarchy, and our own interests as well as theirs forbid it – Nothing that we have done has taught them to govern themselves, we are merely teaching them to co-operate with us under our guidance ... Moreover I doubt if Asiatics will ever learn to govern themselves, it is contrary to the genius of their race, of their history, of their religious systems that they should – Their desire is a mild, just and firm despotism; that we can give them.[18]

The innumerable small and tiny islands of the Melanesian, Polynesian and Micronesian archipelagos did not escape the share-out but were swept up by the imperial broom into British, French or German possession. They had no great material resources to offer, but stations on shipping routes were not unimportant and their male populations were available for recruitment, by voluntary or compulsory means, as labour supply in other parts of the empires.

South America

In the southern portion of the opposite hemisphere there was only one formal British colony, the important sugar-producing British Guiana, but the ostensibly independent states of South America formed both a cardinal element in the network of global financial and commercial dominance and contained the most massive concentration of overseas British capital to be found anywhere – not excluding the settlement colonies.

The last of the great pre-industrial commercial wars[19] ended in 1815 with the unquestionable and unchallengable ascendancy of British commercial capital around the world, aggressively seeking fresh opportunities and new fields for expansion. The decrepit Spanish and Portuguese empires offered tempting prizes, once they could be transformed into independent states maintaining close commercial, political and cultural links with Britain. The states that came into being were indeed British proteges, being protected by the British navy and British diplomatic efforts from any threatened reconquest by the Iberian monarchies. Moreover, in Chile and even more so in Argentina, the new ruling classes of landowners and foreign-trading merchants did absorb, to an extraordinary degree, British economic and cultural values of a liberal but anti-democratic sort. Repression of the independently minded gaucho frontiersmen and extermination of the still-unsubdued Amerindians in Argentina were policies seen as essential to the unity and stability of the new state and pressed upon its rulers by London.

Brazil, whose political form was at first a monarchy – which pleased the Foreign Office – and whose social structure at independence was founded upon slavery – which did not – was a slightly different case, though the outcome in the end amounted to much the same thing. The British forced the Brazilian government to outlaw the slave trade (though it continued to be practised illegally) and ultimately pressured it into abolishing slavery as an institution (as late as 1888). These measures enormously increased the leverage that the Foreign Office had over the governing Brazilian elite, since it became its only reliable upholder in the face of outraged Brazilian landowners who resented the interference with the slave system, and of the Brazilian educated classes who resented the subordination of their country. In 1889 the monarchy was overthrown and succeeded by a republic. Similar relations continued with the new authorities. According to Cain and Hopkins, 'despite its long association with the Brazilian monarchy, the City did not allow sentiment to extend to the point of backing a loser'.[20]

However, in the first half of the century, despite gratifying political success, the chronic crisis of the British economy between 1820 and 1850 during its transition from a hand-manufacturing to a machine-industry mode, reacted upon foreign trade and resulted in severe disappointments so far as South America was concerned: considerable investments were lost. Matters changed dramatically in the second half as railway construction provided both transport systems and opportunities for what had become relatively safe investment. Brazilian rubber and coffee, Argentinian beef and wheat, Chilean copper and nitrates then flowed towards Britain and Europe in an ever-expanding stream, providing further opportunities for shipping, services and investment.

These commercial opportunities, however, were entirely outshone by those created from government borrowing in the South American republics. This indeed was the crucial relationship and the lever by which their governments, regardless of political complexion, were controlled from London. 'Control' in this instance did not mean close supervision on the ground, but a commitment to continue interest payments and maintain the open trading system, imposing only moderate duties on trade sufficient to finance the administration and meet the debt payments but not to interfere with foreign operations. The ability to raise loans in London was regarded as the most vital of lifelines for the South American oligarchies and no government would have dared to act in a manner likely to damage its credit rating in London. There is no reason to think that this dependency was even greatly resented by the elites of the republics, so thorough had been their absorption of British cultural values, though on occasion, when financial crisis had produced the danger of default, anxiety was expressed that force might be employed by the British navy to rectify the situation. American observers and diplomats would grumble that Buenos Aires or Valparaiso were English cities in everything but name and language. From the point of view of the British investor, the British diplomat or the British politician, it was the best of all possible worlds: the conditions of profitability maintained by reliable and accommodating European-descended local authorities and requiring no embarrassing demands upon the British taxpayer – 'honorary dominions' – the kind of set-up that would have been acclaimed in Africa or China had the possibilities existed. That the possibilities did not exist is the essential reason why imperialism in the eastern hemisphere took the shape that it did. The idyllic investment conditions in South America served as the foundation for a debt burden that crushed the Argentinian cattlehand, the Chilean miner or, in the most ghastly instance, the Brazilian Indian rubber-tapper toiling in conditions of indescribable degradation.

The commodity trade between Britain and South America was very considerable – Argentine exports to Britain in 1913, for example, exceeded those of any settlement colony. Nevertheless, Britain's share of the commodity trade with the continent was under continual pressure from rivals in the later part of the nineteenth century and during the years up to 1914: in fact it experienced steady decline. Partly it was a result of British firms themselves shifting their operations to the formal empire. This, however, represented no great problem from the point of view of British finance, for it continued to carry, finance and insure the operations being conducted by the intrusive German or US merchants. In fact, even as commodity trade was declining, London's financial stranglehold on the southern republics was as steadily increasing, and German and US capital, though they tried, proved utterly incapable of shifting British control of the banking systems in the three states.

Turkish and Persian Empires

As with South America, it was during the earlier part of the nineteenth century that the quasi-feudal Turkish empire became a diplomatic satellite of Great Britain. The empire was administratively, politically and militarily decayed, and without British intervention would have been obliterated before too long by the southern expansion of the Tsar's empire and the defection of rebellious provincial satraps.

British intervention on its behalf was expressly designed to obstruct Russian advance towards the sensitive middle eastern route to India and the Pacific, and maintainance of its integrity (more or less) became one of the central principles of British foreign policy.[21] It was hoped too that as a by-product of British diplomatic influence administrative reform and a liberal commercial regime would generate expanded trade relations.

Commodity exchange in fact remained very modest, but following the Crimean War – an episode in the Anglo-Russian conflict – extensive foreign borrowing was embarked upon by the sultan's regime. Funds were attracted from London and Paris, but a dramatic turning-point in Turkish affairs occurred in 1876 when the Ottoman government defaulted on its foreign debt. Consequences were severe. To restore its creditworthiness the regime had to surrender economic sovereignty to a consortium of creditor nations, which proceeded to establish on Turkish territory the Ottoman Public Debt Administration to collect the revenues themselves.[22] Meantime, the North African provinces, in reality autonomous but still Ottoman in international law, were being detached by Britain and France.

However, this political hulk, an imperial authority keeping itself in being by massacre and pillage practised on its own subjects, though of more than trivial importance commercially, was of much greater interest to the

British military and diplomatic service than to British investors. In fact the Foreign Office would have liked to attract more investment than the City was willing to subscribe, in order to reinforce its political influence – influence which it lost in any case with the modernising Young Turk revolution of 1908, being unable in this instance to carry out the same manoeuvre as was to succeed temporarily in China. It was not until it became apparent shortly before 1914 that the southern Ottoman provinces were awash with oil that investors began to prick up their ears in a serious manner, upon which Whitehall gladly extended to them financial and diplomatic support. It was, of course, these same provinces which Britain claimed as its prize after the Turkish defeat in World War I.[23]

To the east the Persian empire, afflicted with a similar but even less commercially promising regime, received similar treatment. First coming under British surveillance, like the Turkish empire, on account of its geographical relationship to India and concern that its collapse could bring Russian power to the Indian Ocean, it stubbornly failed to attract more than a very modest investment, in spite of Foreign Office encouragement of the Imperial Bank of Persia founded by distinguished empire financiers, including officials from Jardine Mathieson and the Hong Kong and Shanghai Bank. As with the Arab provinces of the Ottoman empire, realisation of what was to be found underneath the soil transformed the perception, though in this case Britain was obliged to agree to a formal partition of the country with its new ally, Russia.[24] Following the war and the fall of Tsardom, British capital inherited complete control of the country's mineral resources, and from 1919 Persia was as much a lightly disguised British economic and political colony as were Jordan or Iraq.

Conclusion

Consideration of the pattern of events in Asia and Latin America over the decades in question shows at first glance a bewildering variety of actions, motives and responses by the imperial powers, Britain in particular. The straightforward territorial annexations which occurred, especially on the part of the French, the Dutch, the Russian empire and the new imperial power, Japan, were only the most simple and direct forms of imperial advance. In the main, however, relations tended to be more complicated, and in general the preference was to leave in place a facade of local sovereignty. In Latin America, indeed, there was no alternative, both on account of cultural standards – states under European-descended governments could not be annexed as a rule – and because the United States would not have permitted anything else.

Indeed, the essence of imperial political relations in this era, the standard practice, so to speak, can be regarded as forcing formally independent polities to do the bidding of the imperial power or its agents, or better, forcing them into a relationship where the imperial will is carried out because matters have been so arranged that it appears to be perfectly natural and nothing else is conceivable. Historical perception of the imperial climax has in a way been distorted because events in Africa, and tropical Africa in particular, have featured so prominently in the foreground, created a spectacle both at the time and for the history books, and culminated in sovereignty being seized by a European power, usually Britain. The quieter (though predatory enough) imperialism practised elsewhere around the globe was much more typical – and more related to manifest economic considerations.

If we disregard the settlement colonies and India, which had entered the imperial orbit at an earlier period, the perfect dependencies were the Latin American states, tied to primary production, punctiliously delivering to Britain supplies of foodstuffs and raw materials, serving as absorbers of investment capital to the great profit of commodity traders and the City, paying off their debts (sometimes with a measure of encouragement) and requiring little or no intervention to ensure that their internal regimes maintained the conditions which allowed these unequal relationships to continue undisturbed.

The rulers of Latin America and Japan understood what was required of them; those of China to a much lesser degree, and the scale of intervention to secure European expectations was correspondingly greater. We can see in the case of China, perhaps more than anywhere else, a direct and visible link between the demands of merchants and financiers (and missionaries) and the action of governments. It is not unreasonable to conclude that this was the case because on the one hand the economic importance of China to the west was great and its potential believed to be even greater; on the other, because of the authority that the regime continued to maintain over its subjects, as long as it could be manipulated the amount of European intervention required could be kept within limits acceptable to their exchequers. The British position differed from that of its imperial rivals only in so far as it was more concerned to maintain the integrity of the ramshackle monarchy – Britain stood to lose most if it collapsed or suffered partitioning. However, not least because of popular resistance to European commercial penetration and the enormous cultural divide, the situation in China, in contrast to that in South America, was inherently unstable and constantly subject to the danger of elemental popular rebellion aimed at expelling the foreigners.

In Persia and the Arab world matters differed significantly and there capital (until there appeared the prospect of profits from oil) showed a signal reluctance to risk its fortunes. On the contrary, the picture is one of governments urging financiers, without great success, to commit themselves in that region. Without any doubt the concerns of the British state were strategic ones, and the notion of any economic dimension appears unsustainable. However, the concept of 'strategic' only begs the question what is strategy *about* and what are strategic interests strategically defending?[25]

It is necessary instead to stand back and view the picture globally. Smoothly functioning free-trade imperialism in South America and the settlement colonies, tight control over the Egyptian economy and administration, a regime of unabashed colonial exploitation in India, loans to and concessions wrung from the Chinese emperor, colonial war and conquest in Africa, together with the economic interactions which industrialised nations conducted within and between themselves, comprise a prodigiously complex interlocking structure involving states, empires, mighty centres of population, migrant labourers and nomadic peoples in the furthest corners of the earth, and amount in sum to a regime of accumulation embracing the globe but with its centre in London.

Further Reading

P.J. Cain and A.G. Hopkins, *British Imperialism: Innovation and Expansion 1688–1914*, Longman, 1993.

E.W. Edwards, *British Diplomacy and France in China 1895–1914*, Clarendon, 1987. Fullest examination of this theme.

C.C. Eldridge, *Victorian Imperialism*, Hodder & Stoughton, 1978.

V.G. Kiernan, *The Lords of Human Kind*, Weidenfeld & Nicolson, 1969.

David McLean, *Britain and her Buffer State: The Collapse of the Persian Empire 1890–1914*, Royal Historical Society, 1979. The only book-length analysis of this development.

A.J. Stockwell (ed.), *Cambridge Illustrated History of the British Empire*, Cambridge University Press, 1996.

4

The Evolved Imperial Structure

The British empire actually attained its widest geographical extent following World War I and the victors' decision to reward themselves with confiscated German and Turkish possessions. It appeared briefly that the goals of the epic struggle with Germany to dominate the global circuits of production, trade and finance had been successfully accomplished; the investments in blood and treasure had paid off, so that, with the threatening competitor overthrown, Britain now had an absolutely clear field and business could continue as usual in both senses of the term. It was all the more galling, therefore, to discover that the system itself had toppled into a state of parlous collapse marked by permanent recession and slump and that a new and even more threatening competitor had appeared in the shape of the United States.

Even as the empire reached its zenith, its heyday was past, and historical perspective makes it clear that the height of combined size and influence was to be found in the brief phase before 1914 when the partition of the globe had been completed and the struggle for repartition had not yet descended into a desperate bloodbath. How, therefore, at its apogee was the empire organised? How did the mechanisms which sustained it economically, politically and culturally actually function?

At first sight the British empire of 1910 or thereabouts had no structure at all but was instead a confused and bewildering jumble of self-governing white-settled territories (the term 'Dominions' still lay in the future); colonies with a variety of relationships to Westminster; protectorates of various shapes, sizes and conditions (the key member of this group, Egypt, not even being defined as such); and areas of greater or lesser informal influence – round the Kafkaesque paper maze in which politicians, bureaucrats and diplomats scurried endlessly and often uncomprehendingly.

The Economic Framework

Closer inspection, however, soon reveals a well-articulated structure, to which formal constitutional niceties are largely, if not quite wholly, irrelevant. The empire was designed to fulfil certain clearly defined purposes. In the first place it linked consumption and productive industry in Britain with the wider world by ensuring a constant supply of imported foodstuffs and raw materials upon which the population and the manufacturing process depended absolutely. This it attained not only by including areas of supply within the formal empire, for though important, that was secondary. What was primary was that the empire underpinned the regime of free trade through which imports could be obtained anywhere on favourable terms in exchange for British production.

British production, however, did not cover the full value of import demand, indeed it had not done so since the eighteenth century. To balance the permanent trade deficit which resulted and to show the overall profit which was the starting point of yet further accumulation, the economy relied upon 'invisible earnings', from shipping, agency, banking and insurance services, and increasingly, as the nineteenth century progressed, investment income. The global network of trade and investment, the joint creation not only of Britain but all the developed states[1] formed the soil on which the invisible profits grew, but the empire and the navy which guarded it was well understood to be the guarantee of British capital's privileged access to its cultivation. Possibly, it was thought, it might even guarantee the network's existence, for should Britain's stewardship be removed the intricate mechanism might well be disrupted in a ferocious contest for dominance among powers who had less than centuries experience of these matters.

British global power, both financial and military, therefore extended the late nineteenth century regime of accumulation to parts of the world where it was hitherto unknown or rudimentary; it guarded its continuance once in place and it perpetuated a structured market in which the citizens of any civilised or would-be-civilised nation were welcome to compete but in which the British had a built-in advantage. Other states were no less conscious of the relationship and as the century wore on began to resort to tariffs and protectionist measures in an endeavour to redress some of the balance; not only countries such as Germany whose rulers aspired ultimately to take Britain's place, but also those who had lost hope of doing so, such as France, and those not yet ready to enter the contest, like the United States.

An additional motivation might therefore occur during this period to induce annexation of a tract of territory with commercial potential which was in danger of being absorbed by a protectionist state and thereby ceasing to be a site of British enterprise, if circumstances suggested that was the only recourse to keep it out of protectionist hands – especially if strategic or missionary concerns could also be plausibly argued. The central principle observed in Westminster, however, remained one of minimal interference. The settlement colonies were safely within the sphere of capitalist relations and free trade, so far as capital flows (if not material goods) were concerned – then allow them all the political autonomy they demanded. The Japanese were progressing in the right direction faster than anyone would have imagined to be possible – then sustain them with applause, encouragement and diplomatic blessing. The Chinese state was a lot shakier, but a good borrower and the most likely polity for preserving the open door and the British investment – the keep a close eye on it, but do whatever might be possible by loan and agreement with other powers to preserve its integrity. The Egyptians regrettably could not be trusted on their own to uphold their responsibilities for debt repayment and the protection of the Suez Canal, so unfortunately it was necessary to teach them a short military lesson and subject them to political and military supervision, but their puppet monarch should still be responsible for the tax collection and local administration. Private enterprise could be left to the conquest of the 'savages' (but likely future customers and labourers) of northern Nigeria or the Rhodesias. Even with the obstinately obdurate, such as Boer intransigents, once they were made to yield to the decisive argument of the imperial forces and see sense on the vital issue of unimpeded capital operations, an extensive measure of self-government could be tolerated.

All this is not to argue, as certain historians have done, that the British state and individual administrations of the 1870–1914 period were disinclined to an imperial stance and only very reluctantly expanded the dimensions of the British empire. On the contrary, their disposition was actively and aggressively imperial. What they preferred to avoid if possible was certain more expensive forms of imperial relationship[2] – thought they did not hesitate to assume them if the preferred alternatives were unavailable. The formal empire then must be viewed as simply one instrument among others or one element of a system whose purpose was the extraction of a global surplus. The multiplicity of formal relations between the 'mother country' and the diverse and variegated bits and pieces of the structure have to be viewed primarily as ad hoc and pragmatic responses to the necessity in the different instances to devise a cheap and efficient machinery to institute and protect surplus extraction.

Settlement Colonies

In the settlement colonies the labour power of British-descended males was relatively scarce and consequently, by the standards of the nineteenth century, highly paid. That, of course, was the source of attraction to emigrants. Conditions of employment might still be very harsh and exacting – the life of a Canadian logger or fisherman, of a South African gold miner or of an Australian stockman was certainly no bed of roses. In the case of Canada the surviving and dispossessed aboriginal population was little drawn upon as a labour resource, but that was far from being the case in Australia[3] – which before 1900 consisted of a number of separate colonies – or New Zealand. On the Australian sheep stations minimally rewarded aboriginal labour in all sorts of capacities, some requiring advanced levels of skill, formed a routine component of the workforce. Their payment could be depressed below even basic subsistence because of the links they maintained with kin still outside the market economy, whose support covered the difference. By contrast with North America or Australia, the conquest of New Zealand left the indigenous Maoris a comparatively high percentage of the resulting population. A Polynesian-descended people with an already advanced culture by the time of the European arrival, they were rapidly integrated into the market economy and the labour market. Maoris toiled on farms, in the construction industry, in the docks and on the railways, forming a pool of cheaper labour, excluded from higher-paid occupations and fomenting sectional divisions in the workforce.

The South African case was, however, unique and in a class of its own. The Dutch farmers of the eighteenth century had openly practised agricultural slavery, using captive members of the African population as its victims. Among the principal reasons for the establishment of the Boer republics in the first half of the nineteenth century had been the abolition of legal slavery throughout the British empire in 1832, with the Boers endeavouring as a consequence to escape from British authority at the Cape and perpetuate their system in a location further north. The mineral discoveries in the later part of the century transformed the labour market, as so much else in South African life. Operations in both diamond and gold mines were absolutely dependent on a plentiful supply of African labour in the most menial and dangerous of tasks – it was a resource without which the mines could not have functioned.

While the mining corporations were indifferent in principle as to what colour of skin did which work, and would have been only too pleased to reduce the excessive rewards of white skilled labour by means of black competition, nonetheless it was in their interest to keep African labour-power cheap by compelling the labourers as far as possible to retain a rural connection and especially to keep their families there, surviving on subsistence agriculture, so that the wage costs of an adult male worker did not have to cover the indefinite maintainance of his family as well – in other words to impose upon them the status of migrant workers and deny them residence rights in the mining areas. It was a point of view which coincided nicely with that of the authorities, no less anxious to avert the development of an established black proletariat around the main concentrations of population within their states. Compelled by poverty and overcrowding in the rural areas to which they they were confined to seek paid employment in the mines and accept the erosion of the indigenous social fabric which it occasioned, the black labour force was herded in off-duty hours into vile and insanitary compounds where its members were then unavoidably the victims of violence, petty crime, adulterated provisions and traffickers in the low-grade alcohol which afforded them transient release from their miseries at the same time as contributing mightily to the violence and disorder. It was a repetition of all the worst features characteristic of early industrialisation in Europe or North America, infinitely worsened by the addition of unconstrained racial oppression and cruelty.

Still it was not enough. The Rand mines, producing at full capacity after the tiresome restrictions of the Transvaal government had been removed by the Boer War, had become yet more centrally important to a world financial system established upon the gold standard. Output expanded and the demand for labour grew insatiable beyond even the capacity of impoverished African villages to supply. The answer was sought in indentured Chinese labour, 'coolies' signed up into effective slavery for a specified period of years, shipped to South Africa and confined in even fouler conditions than their African counterparts. The mineowners wanted to recruit 100,000; two years after getting authorisation from the British government they had nearly 50,000, creating what one historian indicted as 'moral sinks of indescribable human beastliness'[4] before the trade was stopped by the incoming Liberal administration of 1906. Most of these contract slaves were eventually repatriated, although a significant Chinese community was left behind in South Africa; in later decades to become victims of apartheid legislation. The import into South Africa of racially stigmatised labour was not confined to the Chinese: Indians were also brought in, not in this case to the mines but mainly to work the sugar plantations of Natal, to work for pay and conditions which no white immigrant would suffer and for which an African workforce could not be found; subsequently they gave rise to a large and politically important community.

Other Areas

The surplus extracted from the formal and informal empire, with a few though important exceptions such as South African minerals, rested overwhelmingly, either directly or in the last analysis, upon agriculture.[5] This was true even of the profits derived from transport systems, for in the main it was agricultural products or raw materials which were shipped; or those from imposed indemnity or borrowing by non-European rulers, for it was on the backs of peasant taxpayers that the repayments were loaded as a rule.[6] In a few instances it might be those of miners of silver, copper, sulphur, coal or other minerals – and in the twentieth century Azerbaijani or Iranian oil workers. From these latter enterprises European investors profited twice over, firstly by the dividends realised on the sale of their product and secondly from the taxes they generated, used to meet repayments on the loan agreements entered into by local rulers – the loans in turn normally being used for the purchase of European-produced goods and services.

As noted above, the British government, which assumed an overall responsibility for policing the global system,[7] preferred to leave the collection of these revenues in the hands of the local tyrant, with or without supervision. In relation to the Latin American states it did not really have any choice in the matter: to have declared a formal protectorate over hitherto independent Spanish- or Portuguese-speaking nations would have been regarded as unacceptable by the standards of nineteenth century international relations. That did not, of course, preclude a great deal of interference in their internal politics, visits by gunboats or demands for control over their customs when the debt was defaulted upon. In the end, however, it was naturally the peon, sharecropper or seasonal agricultural labourer or the miner who paid, directly or indirectly in terms of starvation income, squalor, ignorance, disease and truncated lifespan.

Operation of the system at one remove remained true even in a third of India, for in the case of the 'Princely States' such petty autocrats, though subject to British suzerainty, were left with internal autonomy to misgovern their subjects along traditional quasi-feudal lines. Among the methods of raising finance resorted to by the British government in India was the imposition of a salt tax, which compelled consumers to purchase salt only from a government-leased monopoly and prohibited them from obtaining this necessity anywhere else, such as the sea in the case of coastal communities – the repetition of a taxation practice which had famously contributed to the downfall of the French Bourbons in 1789.

Apart from loans to the Indian government, to princely rulers and railway investment, British enterprise in the subcontinent financed various forms of production, principally, though not entirely, agricultural.[8] The two most favoured cash crops were indigo, the basis of an important range of dyestuffs, and tea, which from the 1870s began increasingly to displace the Chinese product in British teacups. The labour force on these plantations was largely composed of women and children, recruited from over-taxed and poverty-stricken villages pleased to be offered any source of additional income, transported to the plantations virtually as indentured labour and obliged to work there in the most abject and appalling conditions. In the case of China, although this country, outside Hong Kong and, to a degree, the Treaty Ports, was never under direct British control, the demand for revenues to meet debt and indemnity obligations, as well as a rising demand for Chinese products on the world market, transmitted themselves to the basic producers, with further deterioration in the incomes and conditions of already hard-pressed rice growers, tea-pickers and domestic silk producers. As with India, for most of the population there were no reserves, and it only required the slightest failure in rainfall, or any adverse weather conditions, to trigger the onset of devastating famines.

Egypt constitutes the clearest example of what was effectively a colony under military occupation but not acknowledged as such. On paper it remained a province of the Turkish sultan, subject to the authority of his representative the Khedive, who conducted the country's affairs with the assistance of British soldiers and officials. The Khedive's administration was by no means an ornament, Cromer, the real ruler of Egypt, worked through it. The first responsibility of that administration was to preserve the civil order which enabled the holders of Egyptian bonds to be paid, the second to collect the revenues which actually paid them. In the end the growing pressure was felt by the *fellahin*, the Egyptian peasantry, a fact recognised even by contemporary comment in Britain. The fertility of the Nile valley poured its tribute into the banks and discount houses of London.

It wasn't only the exactions of the landlord and the attentions of the tax collector that the luckless peasants were compelled to endure. Disregarding the technicalities of the status afforded to them by their presence in the country, the officer class of the British forces stationed there treated it simply as a conquered colony whose inhabitants existed for no other purpose than to serve their whims. A typical outcome was the 'Denshawni Horror' of 1906 indicted in the British press by George Bernard Shaw. A group of officers had gone out shooting in the delta and proceeded to shoot the domesticated pigeons belonging to the peasants of one of its villages, birds which the Egyptians kept as a species of poultry. When the indignant villagers, their pleas ignored, finally remonstrated with sticks, several, including an elderly man, were hung for their impertinence and others condemned to penal servitude for life.

Where the colonial (or 'protectorate') relationship was open and official, as was the case with most of the late nineteenth-century African acquisitions, whether under Westminster or a chartered company, the principal concern of government was to recover from the colony the basic costs of conquest and administration and to integrate it as quickly as possible into the world regime of production and accumulation on terms which favoured British capital in an implicit but not ostensible manner.

Techniques

The first aspect, recovery of conquest and administration costs, required the extraction of cheap or free labour from the Africans. In some cases, where other devices failed, straightforward coercion and forced labour was resorted to: chiefs would be instructed to supply an allocation of their young men for work in road-laying, building or as carriers. However, this was not a favoured technique – it provoked particular resentment and might give rise to unfavourable publicity back in Britain. The preferred method was to impose taxation. In what had been non-monetary economies and where little opportunity existed for steady exchange relations between the conquerors and their new subjects, the only way left available to earn the cash needed to meet the taxation demands was to enter paid employment either with the imposed public authority or else incoming missionary or private employers – on whatever terms they were prepared to offer, which were certainly likely to be less than subsistence.

The approach to the second aspect – economic integration – was likely to differ considerably depending on the geography and climate of the newly acquired colony. In eastern and south-central Africa the subsistence cultivation and cattle herding typical of the peoples of that area were not well designed to yield a surplus easily capable of being turned into commercial profit. At the same time, however, they contained temperate regions to which European settlers could hopefully be attracted and commercial agriculture and cash crops developed. It was, of course, necessary to evict the Africans already on the ground, confine them to the more infertile and unproductive lands and then, when they found these too meagre for their support, hire them cheaply as agricultural labour. Thus the privileged white farms of Southern Rhodesia came into existence. The participants in Rhodes's invasion force which raised the flag over Fort Salisbury were all rewarded, for example, with extensive acres and the promise of more. Thus, too, appeared the exclusive 'White Highlands' of Kenya, where Africans were altogether prohibited from practising their own agriculture. If possible this was an even more scandalous proceeding than the Rhodesian example, in that the 'legal' basis for the acquisition was local treaty rather than conquest, so that breach of trust was practised here as well as robbery with violence.

West Africa represented a very different state of affairs in view of a climate which made significant European settlement an unthinkable proposition. It implied an on the whole somewhat less ferocious colonial regime and an entirely different mode of surplus extraction and economic integration. On the Niger, particularly its delta, the cash crop of palm oil had been substantially developed even before the onset of the colonial era. There were no large plantations. The production of the oil nut was in the hands of African peasant farmers and the surplus was extracted from them by the Royal Niger Company and the smaller trading enterprises through price differentials. The farmers had to endure additional rake-offs from taxation and protection payments to local bigwigs, but compared to their counterparts in Egypt or eastern Africa their situation was a relatively fortunate one. A very similar set-up prevailed in the southern part of the Gold Coast, the future Ghana, only here the crop in question was cocoa beans rather than palm oil.

The West African economic environment did not provide enormous scope for investment compared with other parts of the colonial or semi-colonial world. There were no weak governments in the style of the Chinese or Latin American to be force-fed with increasingly oppressive loans. Scope for extending the acreage of oil nuts or cocoa beans was limited: some investment was possible in the processing machinery, particularly of the former, but beyond a certain point an enterprise like the Niger Company had to diversify in order to achieve growth. Banking was an attractive option and investment in the administrative infrastructure was a possibility, but not likely in this case to be a source of enormous profits. British West Africa, though not without its economic attractions, failed to provide the opportunity for the sort of returns capable of being realised in central and South Africa, and even more so in Egypt, which was not even a formal colony. The reason is clear – particular conditions made it less practicable to squeeze the basic producers in the manner which could be more readily undertaken in thickly crowded Egypt, temperate South Africa or the grasslands of the east and centre.[9]

Ethnic Diasporas

The institution of long-range migrant contract labour has already been noted. Its importance cannot be overemphasised and it was intrinsic, by the levelling out particular and immediate labour shortages, to making the empire a working and profitable proposition. It would have made it more profitable still but for the social and political resistance developed against it – and with distinct racist overtones – by white labour in Australasia. Nevertheless, Chinese workers did appear in the sugar plantations of tropical Australia to do work for which whites could not be recruited. The Malayan rubber plantations were another enterprise which led to the appearance of an alien Chinese community in a British colony because a suitable local labour force could not be recruited, and of course its members did not remain confined to the plantations.

The Chinese were not recruited from a British colony, but the ease with which they could be hired compared with, for example, Japanese, is indicative of the conditions prevailing in China, both as a measure of the desperate poverty which could bring so many to sell themselves into virtual slavery, and the loss of control over or disregard for its own subjects by the Peking government. India, which *was* a British colony, constituted the other principal source of migrant workforces, and if to this is added the rank and file of the Indian army, the contribution to imperial security and prosperity of these uprooted individuals is incalculable.

Indian migrant labour was shifted even further afield than Chinese. It is to be expected that large numbers would appear on the opposite side of the Indian Ocean, in South Africa, particularly Natal, where sugar plantations required labour. In the words of one authority, 'the sugar planters ... found that Native labour lacked the stability and persistence that sugar planting required'[10] – and although they tried they could not induce the authorities to institute forced labour for the Africans. The case of Kenya was a little more complicated. Indentured labourers – 32,000 of them – were imported in the 1890s to construct the railway to Uganda, but these were swiftly expelled again following its completion, and the ancestors of the subsequent Indian community were enticed on their own initiative, coming over to serve in the areas of petty trade and domestic employment. Indians as well as Chinese were shipped to northern Australia as indentured labour on the sugar plantations in these places,[11] and when this neo-slave trade was at its peak, even as far as South America. Sugar cane in the West Indies was worked with African-descended labour as it had initially been in British Guiana, the colony on the South American mainland, but when the opportunity arose, the African workforce was deliberately replaced in the late nineteenth century for the same reason as the Natal planters sought Indian labour: it was regarded as being both more diligent and more controllable – for in the larger West Indian colonies freed slaves had taken advantage of available land to leave the plantations and set up as petty farmers on their own account. Overall, throughout the empire the numbers involved were enormous. An outstanding case was Malaya, where between 1880 and 1911 Chinese and Indian immigration changed the balance of population from 80 per cent indigenous Malay to 51 per cent.

Another area in which the overall imperial economy could scarcely have functioned without Chinese and Indian labour was in long-haul merchant shipping where Chinese and Indian crew members were universal – naturally being confined to the most menial and worst-paid functions on ship. Even the South Pacific islands, not having much in the way of material resources to exploit (though there were some sugar and copra plantations on the larger islands) could not escape having to make their contribution to the labour tribute. For a time the usual procedure was simply to kidnap these *kanaks* and take them away under duress, again mainly for the convenience of the north Australian sugar growers; later contract labour became the norm, which had the advantage of preventing the victims becoming permanently resident if the employers and the authorities wanted to insist on repatriating them at the end of the contract, which in Australia they always did.

On every continent and upon the oceans connecting them productive energies were exercised in an incalculable variety of functions by a medley of workforces, the majority of whom, excepting the favoured racial elite, toiled in atrocious conditions upon the margins of subsistence. Their output coalesced into a system of global exchange structured by a formally unregulated world market with intrinsic advantage located in western Europe, the United States and the settlement colonies. On top of that was erected a gold – i.e. sterling regulated – system of multilateral exchanges and financial structure of staggering complexity, the net effect of which was to give ultimate title of ownership of a very large part of the structure – and the claims to income derived from that ownership – to interests located principally in the City of London. The formal empire was a part, and possibly not the most important part, of that complex, a historic accretion of territories brought under direct British ownership for a chain of contingent reasons stretching back to the seventeenth century when the English ruling class first set out to dominate the world economy. Once in existence, however, particularly in conditions of intensifying national and international friction, it was soon to acquire a political, social and ideological momentum of its own.

Power and Arms

Titles to ownership, however, are not of much value unless they can be enforced – as investors in Russia discovered after 1917 – and enforcement was a central purpose, indeed it might be claimed *the* central purpose of the imperial structure. It was not so much the enforcement of each and every particular title that was paramount as the maintenance of the overall structure through which claims and titles were enabled to function. Other European powers, even when engaged in colonial rivalry, could usually be relied upon to respect a property title,[12] but the uncivilised, like the unwashed at home, might endanger them at any time by revolt or anarchical conduct. 'Civilised' powers – generally France or Russia – might threaten to exclude British interests from particular slices of territory yet unclaimed, or in due course, in the case of Germany, appear to menace British ascendency over the global system.

A military machine of unparalleled scope existed to avert such dangers from whatever quarter, much of it paid for and staffed by the colonial subjects themselves. By continental standards the British professional army was tiny and specifically designed for holding colonial populations in subjection.[13] British governments preferred to use it in only the most sparing and niggardly fashion and with the onset of the South African war recruiting campaigns had immediately to be put in hand to supplement it with volunteers. Most of the army was stationed in India, partly to overawe the subject peoples and discourage any inclination to revolt on the part of these overwhelmingly numerically superior masses;[14] partly in view of suspected Russian intentions on the northern frontiers.[15] To provide the British rulers with a land army comparable to the conscripted forces of other powers, Indian recruits were relied upon and were centrally placed for use in the subcontinent itself, Africa, the Middle East or eastern Asia. The expenses came out of the budget of the government of India and the financial burdens were sustained by the Indian taxpayer.

Co-ordinating with the Indian army, and of even greater importance in asserting the British world hegemony, was the Royal Navy. Since the seventeenth century superior seapower had been the foundation of the country's imperial strength. It protected all the critical trade routes connecting Britain from interruption, but could easily cut enemy ones; it threatened unchallengable blockade against any European or other enemy, while safeguarding the shipment of troops; if necessary it could be used to bombard recalcitrant seaports and coastlines. Only once, briefly during the nineteenth century when steam-driven ironclad rendered obsolete all the nations' wooden navies, had that awesome superiority seemed in any jeopardy, but it did not take the British long to establish an unbeatable lead in iron as formerly in wooden warships. Although the self-perception of the British public was that their state, without military conscription, was pacific in outlook and, unlike its German or even French rivals, abhorred militarism, in reality British taxpayers paid two and a half times as much for defence as their French or German counterparts.

A further implication of Britain's hegemonic position on the oceans was that all lesser overseas empires, French, German, Dutch or Portuguese, continued only on British sufferance. It was a point too obvious to require emphasising and embodied in the conception of the 'two-power standard', the doctrine which stipulated that the British navy must be bigger and stronger than the next two most powerful navies combined. As we shall see, it was the determination of the German ruling class to challenge this relationship which marked an important milestone on the road to the clash of empires in 1914.

'Regions Caesar Never Knew': Empire and Ideology

This particular theme is so boundless – like the empire itself – that ideally it requires a further volume to itself. What is striking is the speed with which imperial ideology colonised the public discourse and corrupted the civic culture.

In one aspect it represented a continuation and extension of the national chauvinism, peculiarly English but capable of drawing the differently inflected Scottish culture into its orbit, that had been nurtured for centuries as a means of cementing together the gaping social rifts that separated the privileged from the less privileged, and they again from the 'swinish multitude'. It was a form of consciousness perfected during the revolutionary and Napoleonic wars and one that had performed sterling service against English and Scottish Jacobins – stigmatised as tools of the national enemy – reformers, Owenites and Chartists. The imperial ideologues of the 1870s onwards were drawing their raw material from a deeply poisoned well, and more immediately they were elaborating themes which Lord Palmerston had exploited with devastating effect from the 1840s to the 1860s in enhancing his political career.

A pre-existing arrogant conviction of national superiority and of the world-policing role embodied in the British navy, concentrated no doubt in the middle classes but running through all social strata, formed the bedrock upon which the edifice of late nineteenth-century imperialist consciousness was erected. When world economic and political developments placed on the agenda the issue of dividing up the spaces on the map not hitherto subject to close European control, it was easy enough, through the media of the time, to gain public acceptance of British claims, demands and actions as a natural extension of the national moral superiority already responsible for Britain's world lead in industrial output, trade or naval power – the country's particular manifestation of manifest destiny.

Moral Self-congratulation

It scarcely required official initiatives by the imperial power to establish a climate of moral superiority in British popular sentiment, a climate that intensified during the century's closing decades. It found expression through the press, popular entertainments, Sunday sermons, political discourse, the schoolroom, children's literature. In presenting the British empire as a humanitarian institution the examples of revered missionaries such as David Livingstone were strenuously evoked; and the suppression in British India in the early nineteenth century of the form of human sacrifice termed sati (suttee), the practice in Hindu culture of burning widows alive,[16] and other morally unacceptable traditions, was a mighty source of self-congratulation – though on the other hand British rule in India may actually have strengthened the caste system, by adopting uncritically the Brahmin interpretation of Hindu law and putting the force of the colonial power behind it. The British state had also taken the lead, first in formally outlawing the Atlantic slave trade by international treaty in 1807, and then slavery itself throughout its domains in 1832.[17]

Britain, which had been in its time the most energetic practitioner of slave trading, became in the nineteenth century the most zealous of all states in its suppression, and even maintained a West African squadron to catch foreign vessels illicitly plying the trade and naturally awarded itself enormous moral credit for its actions. The motives for this reversal are still disputed.[18] Evidently it would not have happened had West Indian slavery continued to be regarded as vital to the Atlantic economy but given that condition there is no need to question the sincerity of the abolitionists' intentions. Anti-slavery became part of the British official mind and the consequences were far-reaching.

On the Atlantic the British Navy energetically pursued slave traders all along the coast of tropical Africa. Humanitarianism was combined with the practical necessity of not allowing French, Spanish or Portuguese colonies in the Americas to gain a competitive edge by continuing to import slaves. The Sierra Leone colony was established to accommodate slaves freed on the high seas. The Niger delta had been the principal source of supply for the Liverpool slavers. Once the trade was banned the firms involved did not give up. 'Legitimate' commodities were sought to replace it and a profitable one was found in palm oil, which in the later nineteenth century became the basis for most British-produced soap. Thus was the nucleus established of the later Nigerian colony. Interestingly, the British administration there (it took over in 1900 from the chartered Royal Niger Company) was willing to tolerate continued domestic slavery as practised by its more powerful African subjects. In East Africa the results of anti-slavery beliefs and actions were if anything more historically consequential, for by the treaty of 1872 between Bartle Frere and the Sultan of Zanzibar, this outlook had been responsible for beginning the process which brought the area of Kenya, the Lakes and the Nile headwaters under British control.

The conviction that the British empire corresponded more to the idea of a natural phenomenon than a political construct was instiled early in the impressionable consciousness, with the object that was probably the most vivid and colourful feature of the elementary schoolroom – the wall map with the British-owned portions of the world portrayed in brilliant red. The instruction continued with children's and adolescents' imaginative literature, especially that intended for boys, where the exploitation of imperial themes in juvenile fiction, both magazine and book form, was wholly relentless.[19] The empire after all supplied an endless theatre for adventure and excitement: perceptions which were ultimately institutionalised in the Boy Scouts and Girl Guides movements, organisations founded by a colonial general and hero of the South African War, and the activities and rituals of which, particularly the Scouts, took for granted an imperial context. At the other end of the social scale the public schools became virtually interlocked with the empire, advanced from the purpose of homogenising a political and social elite out of the divergent components of the English ruling class to one of training that class to govern an empire.

The Media

The development of the mainstream traditional press during the last third of the century is both instructive and depressing. Whether we are dealing with the London dailies or the major provincial newspapers, the trend is similar. In the 1870s the expressed editorial attitude towards the minor instances of territorial expansion which occurred in that decade is one of caution and reserve. Notions occasionally expressed in favour of an aggressive imperial policy, such at that of Bartle Frere, are reported in a sceptical and ironic mode. By the late 1890s these same journals were gloatingly rejoicing over if Conservative, or accepting in more measured terms if Liberal, the mass slaughter of Sudanese dervishes. The word 'jingo' was coined in the 1870s. It has been pointed out that publishers and publicists, least of all those aiming at a juvenile market, were not dragooned into celebrating imperial themes, but acted for commercial motives. Exactly so. They knew what would sell and responded to the market.

The advent of the popular daily press in the 1890s added a new dimension to the cultivation of chauvinist and imperialist attitudes: these publications did not even make a pretence of arguing the benefits of empire but asserted with strident dogmatism the virtues of imperial conquest and rule[20] and the intrinsic connection between patriotism, empire and the Conservative Party.[21] Rudyard Kipling, Nobel laureate for literature, proclaimed the same sentiments in verse and somewhat more elevated style.[22] The Celtic warrior-queen Boudicca could by hymned (though not by Kipling) as a forerunner of Britain's imperial glory, the poet using her as a pretext for noting the restricted compass of the ancient Roman empire compared with the British present-day one,[23] and of course a fanciful statue was erected to her in the heart of London. Empire exhibitions combined entertainment with instruction in the multifarious lands under the British flag. The jubilees to celebrate the 50th and 60th anniversaries of Queen Victoria's accession were designed, especially that of 1897, no less as celebrations of imperial achievement, with cohorts of subjects of every colour fetched from all around the world to make up a procession in the capital and which resembled – perhaps deliberately – the triumph of a Roman emperor, as well as creating a lively market in souvenirs.

The public rhetoric used to validate imperialism and imperial expansionism both drew on the past and added some late nineteenth century refinements. Supposed material benefits were not ignored, and the assumption was industriously promoted in press and educational materials that imperial links improved access to the range of imports on which the British public was dependent. Whether this was actually the case was not likely to be dispassionately investigated – least of all in the popular media. It was likewise not difficult to argue that the densely populated but geographically restricted offshore island was able to lead the world only because its bounds were extended so enormously across the globe. Neither of these assumptions was altogether vacuous, although both mistook the glitter for the substance and a financial relationship for a political one. Permeating the public consciousness, however, and voiced with growing stridency, were more philosophic justifications for empire.

Attitudes

These justification may be defined as the peculiar ability of Britons to govern inferior races; the associated notions of 'civilising mission'[24] and progress; and the increasingly touted myth of social Darwinism, itself a product of intensifying international, imperial and social struggles.

So far as the first of these was concerned, the British state had acquired lengthy practice in India and the Caribbean and there had been plenty of time for attitudes of innate superiority cultivated among colonial administrators and soldiers to seep down among the general public. Back in the 1830s the historian Macaulay, commissioned to lay out the design for the Indian civil service, insisted that it should be cut to an English template.[25] He was later to gloat, as did the historian and prophet of empire, J. A. Froude, over the suppression of the Mutiny and consequent atrocities. Leading literary figures such as Carlyle and Dickens were no less enthusiastic to applaud the savagery with which the Jamaica insurrection was put down in 1864.[26] Britain, it must be remembered, of the major European powers, had been far more involved than any other in the slave trade, and in India ruled colonial subjects on a scale enormously beyond any other colonising state. With technological advance and social reform during the nineteenth century came the idea of progress, and when this was yoked to a pre-existing assumption of ethnic superiority, the idea of a people uniquely qualified to bring forceful order, enlightenment and civilisation to barbarians and savages around the globe did not take long to follow.

> the Indian canal system could technically have been built at almost any period of known history. What the British added was above all the power of a unified and authoritarian state which acted because it saw the danger of drought and famine to its rule.[27]

The same author notes that institutions such as the British Museum, Natural History Museum, Science Museum and Kew Gardens were not only temples of knowledge but 'memorials to British expansion and acquisitiveness', displaying not only knowledge but 'the confident capacity to control it'.

The British, however, could and did congratulate themselves upon treating the inhabitants of their colonial possessions more humanely than sadistic Latins like the Portuguese or French, the iron-hearted Germans or Boers, or the especially notorious regime of King Leopold's Congo. Kipling, as always, was on hand to draw the moral, insisting that the sole concern of the British administrator in India was with the welfare of his charges: if matters went well this paragon happily stood back to let the Indians take the credit, if they turned out badly he manfully stepped forward to shoulder the blame.

It was a standpoint which, regardless of its shortcomings, at least pretended to concern itself with the welfare and ultimate advancement of the colonised and so was logically incompatible with social Darwinism – the doctrine that races (or nations, or classes) were locked in a zoological struggle for survival or dominance, that the least fit would rightfully suffer extermination[28] and that the coloured ones would serve the white in perpetuity without any nonsense about eventually fitting the former to participate in European civilisation. Logical contradiction did not, of course, prevent both notions being adhered to simultaneously by imperial publicists. In the early twentieth century, as international tensions sharpened and the powers geared up to settle their differences by all-out conflict, the Darwinian interpretation of how the empire should function on behalf of Britain and the settlement colonies began to assume growing prominence in the minds and speeches of leading imperialists.

'Oldest Colony'

The ideology of empire was baleful in every respect, and came home to torment the United Kingdom, with gruesome long-term effects. Between the 1880s and the onset of World War I (and thereafter), the politics of 'Britain's oldest colony', Ireland, were a major destabilising feature in the British political system and constitutional structure, as well as a focus and rallying issue for all the most sinister and reactionary elements in state and society. By 1914 the tensions generated around it looked capable of precipitating civil war.

During the 1870s, underground agrarian violence directed at landlords, memories of famine and revolt, embittered consciousness of centuries of English misgovernment and religious discrimination coalesced, when it became possible to express them in the conditions of franchise extension and secret ballot after 1870, into a political demand for limited self-government – Home Rule – expressed through the eighty or so Irish MPs elected to the Westminster parliament. Violent opposition came from all the forces of the traditional English ascendancy, landlords, officialdom, military, and from the Protestant masses of the north-east, centred on the manufacturing and shipbuilding city of Belfast.

The dispute occasioned a split in the Liberal Party, resulting in twenty years of nearly uninterrupted Conservative government and the defection of an important section of the peerage and of hitherto Liberal industrial-ists and opinion-formers to the Tory ranks.[29] The Conservatives adopted intransigent opposition to Home Rule, along with support for imperial-ism, as their banner and indeed renamed themselves the Conservative and Unionist Party. Seen only from a British perspective the matter was cer-tainly significant enough, and foreshadowed an armed confrontation and possible civil war if the dispute could not be resolved by constitutional methods – which by 1913 looked likely to be the case, as rival armed para-military formations were being organised by the opposing sides in Ire-land.[30] The purely British perspective, however, is not enough. Why, it may be asked, should the Conservatives and their allies so totally identify themselves with the Ulster minority, expect that identification to find a favourable response among the mainland public, and be prepared to go to the brink on behalf of this sectarian minority interest?

Class solidarity between the ruling elites in both islands was no doubt part of the story, but Home Rule did not really threaten the propertied Unionist intransigents in any very material way and certainly not to the extent that it became a choice between civil war and class liquidation. Again, it is pertinent to note that the Conservatives began to view Union-ism as the only instrument left to them for regaining power following the shattering electoral defeats of 1906 and 1910, but the question persists as to why they found it profitable to treat the matter in such a fashion.

The answer can be found in imperialist ideology, both at an elite and popular level. Asquith's Liberal ministers, no less imperialist in practical terms than their parliamentary opponents, were perfectly aware that Home Rule posed no threat whatever to vital imperial interests, regarded it as a distraction and did not hide their impatience with the fact that they were forced to address it only because they were, after 1910, dependent on the Home Rule MPs for their parliamentary majority. Where the difference lay was that the Conservatives, while happy to exploit imperialist senti-ment in a wholly cynical manner whenever it suited them, were never-theless emotionally committed to it in a manner different from the Liber-als. That sentiment was the strap which held together Tory grandees, Ulster Unionist politicians, army and navy officers, Orange hooligans and the Conservative rank-and-file. Home Rule, while it would have conferred on a Dublin parliament fewer powers than those enjoyed by its Canadian, Australian or New Zealand equivalents, represented an intolerable sym-bolic rupture of the unity in the imperial heartland itself; the more so as control of that parliament would surely fall to elements whose loyalty to the imperial ideal was less than sacrosanct and whose acceptance of the British connection was grudging at best.

Ironically, it had proved infinitely easier to arrive at a compact with the defeated Boers and from 1910 to welcome their leaders to power sharing in the Union of South Africa – at the expense of the Africans and other non-white communities. That was a model of how the evolved imperial structure was meant to work, safeguarding this structure and its regime of accumulation, bringing European-descended populations into junior partnership, and retaining vital assets like the Rand mines or the Suez Canal secure under British control of one sort or another. It was instead at the very heart of the enterprise that the contradictions could not be resolved and the fuse was burning towards an explosion.

Further Reading

P.J. Cain and A.G. Hopkins, *British Imperialism: Innovation and Expansion 1688–1914*, Longman, 1993.

P.L. Cottrell, *British Overseas Investment in the Nineteenth Century*, Macmillan, 1975.

L.E. Davis and Robert Huttenback, *Mammon and the Pursuit of Empire: The Political Economy of British Imperialism 1860–1912*, Cambridge University Press, 1986.

C.C. Eldridge, *Victorian Imperialism*, Hodder & Stoughton, 1978.

A.R. Hall, *The Export of Capital from Great Britain 1870–1914*, Methuen, 1968. Comprehensive.

Ronald Hyam, *Britain's Imperial Century 1815–1914: A Study of Empire and Expansion*, Batsford, 1976. Examines the relationship between informal and formal empire.

Paul Kennedy, 'Debate. The Costs and Benefits of British Imperialism 1846–1914', *Past & Present* 125, 1989. Critique of O'Brien, below.

P.K. O'Brien, 'The Costs and Benefits of British Imperialism 1846–1914', *Past & Present* 120, 1988. Argues that imperialism was a drain on British resources.

Jeffrey Richards (ed.), *Imperialism and Juvenile Literature*, Manchester University Press, 1989. Classic analysis of this theme.

A.J. Stockwell (ed.), *Cambridge Illustrated History of the British Empire*, Cambridge University Press, 1996.

5

Imperial Relations

That an explosion did not occur in the British Isles in the manner which seemed likely in 1914 was due to events there being overtaken by the onset of general war in Europe, culmination of the politics of empire and the inter-imperial relationships that had developed over three decades. The empire which entered the conflict – for all King George's possessions and dominions became part of the war machine – was the same free-trade, loosely articulated formation that had evolved into its final form around the turn of the century. A different conception of how the empire might be organised, and the function it could fulfil, was strongly pressed, as we shall see, within the ruling class and on electoral platforms during the twenty years before the outbreak, but had failed to gain political acceptance.

Settlement Colonies

Canada, Australia and New Zealand (South Africa was a somewhat different case) for all their web of economic ties to Britain could not have been compelled to enter the war alongside the state to whose head they were formally subject if these colonial legislatures had decided otherwise, and in that event it would have been unthinkable for the British to have attempted any sort of forceful coercion. It would have been no less unthinkable, however, for any of the three to have held back. To grasp why this was so it is necessary to understand the character of the relations between the settlement elites, the electorates of which they had to take account and the imperial authority to which they looked for geopolitical guidance.

The first point to note is that the economic links were mutually beneficial ones. These areas provided foodstuffs and raw materials to the British market and interest and service payments to the financial apparatus, but equally, as an outlet for their exports and source of loan funds, Britain was indispensable to the settlement colonies. Over the period between 1870 and 1914 the proportion of exports going to the settlement colonies (and Latin America) expanded substantially at the expense of exports to the USA. The shift in emigration patterns was much more marked still. At the start of the period the United States was overwhelmingly the destination of preference and between 1890 and 1900 28 per cent of emigrants went to imperial destinations: between then and 1912 the percentage rose to 63 and in the latter year more emigrants left for Australia than the USA.[1] British defeat in a European war, if sufficiently serious, would have been calamitous for the settlement colonies' economic and consequently political health. All the same, such long-term and relatively abstract considerations would not necessarily be decisive when faced with an immediate question of sending their young men halfway round the world to spill their blood.

Although the men who exercised local rule in the settlement colonies were extremely sensitive to any infringement on what they regarded as areas of concern particular to themselves, they were nevertheless tied to the Westminster government politically as well as economically. Nowhere was this more apparent than in relation to foreign affairs and defence. The colonial ruling elites had absolutely no experience of international relations or diplomacy and had always relied upon Westminster to act on their behalf in dealings with foreign powers. Not even Cecil Rhodes had presumed to negotiate on his own account with Germans or Portuguese. Moreover, the very military protection of these communities and the availability of military power as a bargaining chip in negotiations was entirely within British hands. The Canadians had on their borders an infinitely dynamic and potentially aggressive neighbour in the shape of the United States, which, in the absence of British support and protection, threatened always to reduce them to subservience if not encroach upon their territory. Australia and New Zealand had to some extent the natural protection of distance and isolation, nevertheless in 1905 Japan had decisively defeated Tsarist Russia and revealed itself clearly as an expansionist imperial power. Its range was as yet limited, but who could tell what ambitions it might yet develop in the Pacific? In any case the Germans were already there in New Guinea and the Pacific islands, albeit on a limited scale, but much too close for comfort to British Australasia.

Yet when all these things are taken into account there can be little real doubt that the principal bond between Britain – including the British state – and the settlement colonies was one of sentiment, as it would have been termed at the time, or a feature of identity politics as we might designate it today. No doubt the almost complete autonomy which Westminster accorded them in internal affairs did a lot to reinforce the sense of identification among the settlement colony elites – it removed potential issues of dispute out of which a hostile sense of identity might have been forged.

The most potentially sensitive of these issues had been that of the unallocated lands in the interior of the colonies – enormous reserves of real estate capable of producing vast incomes for their eventual owners and the lenders who advanced funds for their development. Legally these were crown lands, with their ultimate ownership and the right to alienate them vested in the British crown, but no British government ever tried to exercise that putative right, leaving it instead in the hands of the colonial governments. These elites therefore had the best of both worlds – the sense of belonging to the greatest empire in all history and enjoying the protection of the central power but not finding that these circumstances had any adverse implications for what they might wish to do in their own sphere – as late as 1900 the personnel of the Colonial Office consisted of no more than twenty clerks. Since these colonies were also resolutely committed to the world capitalist system with its British leadership and, apart from a few annoyances,[2] to the framework of free trade, Westminster did not have any reason to fear that the autonomy which they were accorded was in any danger of being abused, in the sense of the ruling notions of the period.

The sense of British identification was doubtless strengthened by the fact that up to 1914 the majority of these colonies' inhabitants, both elites and masses, were first or second generation Canadians, Australians or New Zealanders, the end of the nineteenth century having seen the greatest surge of emigration, and so their identity was likely to be in any case felt as a dual one. Modern forms of communication had, moreover, since the beginning of the nineteenth century greatly shrunken the world. The steamship and the telegraph kept the settlement colonies in continuous, indeed daily, contact with Britain, by contrast to the unavoidable isolation to which the seventeenth- and eighteenth-century North American colonies were subject. Formal sovereignty was located in a governor-general appointed in London, the monarch's representative who, like the British monarch, called upon the most favourably placed politician in the colonial assembly to form a government. It was hardly an onerous relationship, and the majority of the white inhabitants of the settlement colonies could get on with making money, bettering themselves, or even, in Australasia, experimenting with social welfare schemes, secure in the knowledge that their economies were well-integrated into the trading and financial network supervised by the world's strongest financial and naval power, which also took care of their defence in the harsh outside world of rapacious militarism.

India

It was a very different story where the monarch's overseas subjects had different skin pigmentation. In the directly governed parts of India the relationship was simple enough – few Indians, regardless of wealth or education, could hope to occupy any but the lowliest of positions in the administration, police or military and the representatives of the Raj, the collectors and magistrates, comported themselves as, in Victor Kiernan's phrase, 'the lords of humankind'.[3] It hardly mattered what view the Indians themselves took of the situation. To quote a cliché, 'resistance was futile':

> The peasants and the tribal peoples who constituted the majority of the population rose repeatedly in rebellion in many parts of the country ... The immediate causes of these risings varied, but most were rooted in the massive dislocations caused by the process of conquest and consolidation. The people driven to rebellion in sheer desperation included peasants forced to give up cultivation during the period of plunder, tribes deprived of their hereditary rights to the free use of forest resources, tenants rack-rented or expropriated by landlords created under the new tenures and cultivators hopelessly indebted to moneylenders (who benefited from the new laws of contract) ... The forces of law and order were almost invariably deployed in favour of their oppressors. The new legal system was incomprehensible and too expensive to be of any use to the poor ... The new equality before the law meant that a Brahmin could now be hanged, but such triumphs of justice were of little consolation to the peasant who lost his land to the moneylender or the landlord ... As late as 1899 famine mortality remained high because vast sections of the population lacked the purchasing power to buy food even when it was available.[4]

Some Indian thinkers nevertheless regarded it as, on balance, a positive development, dragging the subcontinent, however painfully and insensitively, out of its millennia-old superstition and obscurantism; a cognate sentiment was that at least religious faiths of one sort or another were protected from molestation by rival ones. For others, undoubtedly the majority engaged in peasant agriculture and handicraft trades, the Raj was mostly an irrelevance – their forebears were well accustomed to surviving under alien and predatory rulers and the British were merely the latest in a lengthy line – although differing from their predecessors in that their machinery of exaction was incomparably more efficient. Some, the surviving intelligentsia of the old cultures, may have regarded the colonial presence as an outrage and humiliation, but it was clear that pre-British India was gone past recovery, as the Mutiny had fearsomely underlined. In the era of high imperialism any notion of expelling the invader was absent: it had no material surface on which to get a grip, no social element in which it could become embodied and effectively was an idea which could not be thought, the necessary conceptual framework was absent. British rule for the fore-seeable future had come to seem like a fact of nature.

When political organisation among educated Indians did begin to de-velop towards the close of the century in the shape of the Indian National Congress, its initial objectives were very limited, no more than to demand a modest share in governmental authority for suitably qualified Indians, and certainly in no way any kind of challenge to the Raj. It was not until the aftermath of World War I, the Russian Revolution and the Comintern's proclamation in favour of complete colonial liberation,[5] that the question of Indian independence appeared at last on the agenda, to be taken up *af-terwards* by Gandhi and the Congress politicians.

The existence of the princely states, former kingdoms of the Mughal empire whose rulers had seen the wisdom of making treaties subordinat-ing themselves to Company rule before they were forcibly evicted, pro-vided advantages to British control in a number of senses. Most immedi-ately and practically it delegated to these petty monarchs, with British residents on hand to keep them up to the mark, the responsibility for 'main-taining order' and thereby economised on personnel and resources with-out in any way derogating from the Raj's own supreme authority. Secondly, they enabled the imperial government when convenient to avoid respon-sibility whenever it was a question of carrying through progressive mea-sures demanded by public opinion in Britain but which the Raj preferred to avoid. Finally, and in due course, the princely states became a useful lever for dividing the national movement by establishing another inter-est which must be reconciled before any movement would be permissible in the direction of Indian political rights or responsibility. In return the Raj was pleased to underwrite their feudal privileges and condone their misgovernment so long as it did not conflict with British requirements.

Africa and Others

Whether or not we include the special case of South Africa – which com-bined the character of a settlement colony, rule over a numerically supe-rior black helot population and relations with an antagonistic European descended settler community – almost no generalisation can be made about the character of the governing structures prevailing in the African empire except to say that as a general rule with many exceptions the British preferred where possible to work through subordinate African instruments, even going so far in some cases as to create the institution of 'chieftainships' where none had hitherto existed.

The state of affairs in Egypt was the one which most closely replicated that in India – indeed Egypt might almost be regarded as an India in miniature in terms of the realities of the occupation, except that there was no British civil service and the pretence was maintained of an pre-existing Turkish sovereignty, under guidance but not eradicated. The conquest of the Sudan in the 1890s was undertaken under the formal authority of the Egyptian monarch – ultimately that of his 'sovereign' in Constantinople – and the commanding general, Herbert Kitchener, used the Turkish title of 'Sirdar'. As concurrently in India there was nothing around which an independence movement could at that stage focus, certainly not the corrupt and degenerate court. At the end of World War I indeed, with Turkey a defeated enemy power, the Khedive's title was even promoted to that of king and the country officially recognised as an independent state – which did not of course prevent it from remaining as much under British control as before.

In the parts of tropical Africa conquered by Britain or British agents there were some indigenous kingdoms, such as that of the Ashanti north of the Gold Coast, the Baganda beside Lake Victoria, or the Ndebele kingdom north of the Limpopo as well as some emirates and sultanates in the literate Muslim sahel belt north of the Niger, but none of these sovereignties was particularly extensive and most African polities where they existed were very geographically restricted. The normal sort of legalism employed for taking over new territory, whether by an authorised agent of the crown or a freelance entrepreneur was, as illustrated in Chapter 2 with reference to the British South Africa Company or Royal Niger Company, to persuade a chief or potentate to accept a treaty placing his lands and people under the protection of the British crown or chartered company – a treaty which might well also contain clauses relating to mineral and land rights. In some instances, where the African authorities were very fragmented, it might be necessary to collect a stack of such treaties before the desired block of territory to be claimed could be put together and, if necessary, negotiations begun with any contending power.[6] If an indigenous king rather than a petty chief could be got to sign, so much the better; it made for less trouble and fewer bribes. Of course, none of the illiterate signatories, confronted with the novel technologies of pen and paper, had much idea of what they were signing or signing away, and many, wholly unconscious of the mystic significance attached by Europeans to putting handwritten marks at the end of certain texts, no doubt did so as a gesture of courtesy in deference to the peculiar customs of their visitors. When in due course the implications of what they had done became plain, their people might well rise in revolt, with or without their encouragement – which provided the Europeans with a pretext for military action to squash whatever degree of autonomy might have been left in the treaty and, if so minded, seize whatever land took their fancy. Such, for example, was the scenario played out in Matebeleland, which became Southern Rhodesia.

Once established, and with overt resistance subdued, it became general policy, except in the areas marked down for extensive European settlement, i.e. the Rhodesias and Kenya, to disturb the pre-existing social and political order as little as was compatible with extracting whatever surplus might be available from a particular colony. In 1900 government service in the dependent empire, excluding India, employed no more than 1,500 civilian functionaries. A prime consideration was to make the new colony/protectorate pay the costs of its own acquisition and, if relevant, conquest. This could be done through the imposition of taxes, which, as noted above, had the additional advantage of forcing the indigenous population into the labour market. Wealth-producing activities, however, where they existed and could be tapped into by European commerce, were disrupted as little as possible. Thus the aim on the lower Niger was to keep the African peasantry cultivating the oil palm, the economic backbone of the region, and likewise with the cocoa bean on the Gold Coast. The pre-existing indigenous forms of government could be reworked and utilised to attain that objective.

Approaches of this kind could even be worked up into a theory of colonial government for areas where the British presence was expected to be numerically slight. Termed 'indirect rule' by its inventor and proponent, Frederick Lugard, it was a generalisation of his practice in the large area of northern Nigeria, to which he had been appointed governor, and imitated to a degree the model of the princely states of India. It meant the maintenance, where one existed, or creation if not, of an African authority, which would conduct the actual details of government, with British power standing at a distance to ensure that the delegated authority was exercised in an appropriate fashion. The idea was both to economise the resources which the imperial power had to deploy, and to insulate so far as possible sociopolitical relations among the colonised from any economic transformations that their colonial status might be bringing about – in other words to freeze in place an authoritarian traditional or pseudo-traditional administrative structure intended to serve British interests and collect British taxes, using it to exclude from influence Africans who might have developed a modern political consciousness as a result of economic changes and/or European education.

> The scheme of 'indirect rule', which the colonial administrator Frederick Lugard developed in northern Nigeria, became the orthodox method of 'native administration' ... Here political officers conducted local government through African chiefs. Ruling through chiefs triggered a quest for chiefs: in societies where there were no chiefs ... the British created them. In so doing they ... led administrators to advance some ethnic groups over others. In India the British were accused of deliberately highlighting the differences between Hindu and Muslim the better to control them ... In Nigeria political officers favoured the Hausa against the 'coast African'; and the Malay was preferred to the migrant Chinese in Malaya. Collaboration with some was matched with discrimination against others ... Subject peoples were identified as princes or peasants, as warriors or clerks, as nomads or labourers, as Hindus or Muslims, as 'denationalised' (that is, western-educated) or 'real' (that is, uncorrupted by European influences) ... This contributed to the compartmentalisation of colonial societies and the multiplication of communal identities.[7]

Indeed, it was not only in Africa that similar principles were applied, although mostly it was done instinctively rather than in the theorised form developed by Lugard for tropical Africa. A highly significant instance relates to the southern and eastern shores of the Arabian peninsula, where in fact the development of such relationships had commenced much earlier. The fragmented Arab emirates and sheikhdoms on the western side of the Gulf were viewed, not surprisingly, as presenting an inviting target to any power which might be inclined to make trouble for the British position in India. (In the early nineteenth century the power in mind was France.) Consequently, beginning in the 1820s, and by stages throughout the remainder of the century, the feudal dynasts of the region were made offers they could not refuse to place themselves under British protection, which, thanks to the British navy and the Indian army, could be guaranteed without too much difficulty – as could their acceptance. From a commercial or developmental point of view the region was initially worthless, its only value being a strategic one and the British government's only concern being to keep it out of the hands of a potentially hostile power. Consequently, the new relationship had minimal or absolutely no impact on the internal affairs of these petty autocracies.

The opening of the Suez Canal in 1869 and the occupation of Egypt thirteen years later underwrote the farsightedness of the earlier arrangements, as the region was now closely situated near the Red Sea shipping routes,[8] and British hegemony in the Gulf provided an additional security for the canal. When in the course of the twentieth century it became evident that these desert monarchies contained untold riches in the shape of oil beneath their sand, investment came pouring in, and from being peripheral and secondary to the global economic structure the Gulf monarchies rose to become of central importance. Indirect rule here had come to pay unforeseen and handsome dividends, both literally and metaphorically, for with treaty-bound autocrats in charge of affairs, the oil wealth was safe from interference by popular movements or political dissidence growing out of the social transformations generated by the oil extraction industry.

At the other end of the Asian continent the use of similar procedures consolidated the British position in parts of the Indonesian archipelago not under Dutch control.[9] Here again the initial motivation was to control territory useful to cover vital forms of production, in this case Malayan rubber; major trade centres like Singapore; or the Chinese shipping route. Again, however, there proved to be an ultimate payoff of a different kind. The Sultan of Brunei on the island of Borneo is said today to be the wealthiest individual in the world, again as a result of holding property rights to an underground sea of oil.

Clash of Empires

We have already taken note of the rivalry for territorial acquisitions in Africa which first developed during the 1880s between several of the colonial powers, in this case including Portugal, and continued into the twentieth century The same process, though less sharply delineated, was visible in Asia as well, and we now have to examine it in the context of shifts in the global economy and political structure occurring in the years leading up to 1914.

As a result of the communication innovations of the third quarter of the century, telegraph, railway and steamships, all parts of the world except the most remote or inhospitable were bound together into a single world market, although because of transport inadequacies and surviving elements of protectionism, not a wholly perfect one. Nevertheless, the free circulation of goods, capital and, to an astonishing extent, labour as well, marked a tolerably close approximation to the free trade universe conceived by the Adam Smith inspired ideologues of the early nineteenth century, the 'Manchester School', while the same developments, combined with advancing agricultural technologies, had enabled the capitalist mode of production to evade – at least for the Atlantic economies – the Malthusian and Ricardian traps that had haunted the nightmares of the said prophets – namely the fear of population outstripping available food supplies or the rate of return on invested capital falling to zero.

The global system was, however, not an undifferentiated mix of equal actors in the world market, but a highly structured one, completely dominated by the few economies which had made the breakthrough into machine technologies driven by artificial power sources. The fact that there were several economies of this sort rather than just one, and stretching from central Europe across the Atlantic to the eastern seaboard of north America, was indicative that the industrial transformation, though in one sense indifferent to state frontiers, had taken place, as it had to, within state systems required to regulate property and class relations, their role in fact becoming much enhanced as they were compelled to apply themselves to taming and regulating the forces released by the new economic processes which would otherwise certainly tear apart civil society. Capital was thus simultaneously national and international, its representatives not a homogenous transnational class, but British, Germans, French, Americans, with particular state and military connections, systems of law and administration, ideological and cultural outlooks. As the later years of the century wore on, moreover, units of capital tended to grow, through Darwinian processes of growth, extinction and absorption of the less fit in the market struggle and also because size conferred evident advantages in the competitive struggle, both in terms of economic power and political clout.[10]

Capitalism being inherently competitive, it was unthinkable that state power and diplomacy would not be called upon from time to time to supplement the economic search for industrial, commercial or financial opportunities, but this was to introduce further complexity, for capitalist classes are internally divided and competitive as well as nationally differentiated. In addition, no capitalist class, even supposing that a general capitalist will could have been identified, had unfettered control over its own government[11] – which in many cases contained representatives of social groups far from content with capital's generalised ascendancy,[12] and in all cases, whatever its social basis, always developed an official mind of its own detached from particular class interests and had at least to purport to represent a common national interest transcending particular class ones. Lobbying approaches by particular business interests would therefore not necessarily succeed. Nonetheless, although success might not be achieved, there was some point in lobbying one's own government if an individual or company wanted commercial protection or advantage abroad: it was scarcely worthwhile to do the same with a foreign one.

In instituting any particular line of policy on the world stage any government would have to take into account both the complex of internal pressures and forces acting upon it – with its own members simultaneously part of these same forces and standing at a distance from them – and the perils and problems such a policy was likely to encounter both from difficulty of execution and possible hostility evoked on the part of equal or stronger powers. Disparity of military force might of course be neutralised by cunning and diplomacy, as King Leopold demonstrated.

As the reach of the world economy, upon the foundations laid in the third quarter of the century, pressed outwards in the fourth one in spite of – or perhaps because of – the so-called 'great depression', the circle of great powers had a joint interest in bringing the remaining unintegrated portions of the globe – the interiors of Africa and China being the outstanding unfinished business – into full market relationships. They likewise had separate and contradictory interests in securing as much as possible of the new opportunities for their national capital.

This is the context in which the British position has to be evaluated. In the late nineteenth century the structures of international capital revolved, like planets with a sun, round the City of London. The City did not need to have direct direct control or overview of the economies in its orbit: its gravitational attraction, to continue the metaphor, or, more literally, the automatic processes of the gold-based international market, did all that was required. The components of this unique position were many – they included the long experience of international trade, money-dealing and banking for which the City was renowned together with the enormous accumulation of liquid capital from two centuries of successful rapacity and entrepreneurship; the gigantic strength of the industrial economy; the unsurpassable merchant and fighting navies; the integration of the settlement colonies, acquired ad hoc for quite different reasons but by then major world markets in respect of agriculture, services and capital; and India, the 'jewel in the crown'. Eventually South African gold was added, the keystone of the arch, so to speak.

British products might be experiencing growing difficulty in overseas markets – or even British ones – but British capital could go anywhere, and in the years leading up to 1914 increasingly did so. The priority of the British state was to sustain a world order in which this happy circumstance could be made to continue indefinitely. So long as the circuits flowed without impediment and the interest payments were safe, it did not much matter to British finance whose flag flew over any particular part of the world, for the British lender could always compete favourably and was as likely as not to prevail.[13] The colonies and protectorates acquired after 1870 (excepting always the South African Republic) should therefore be seen less as a first-order priority[14] for the imperial system than an insurance policy taken out to keep these parts of Africa and Asia within the open market – the same objective to which policy was directed also in relation to China, the Middle East and Latin America.

It was the weaker or newly emerging imperial powers, with less developed concentrations of national capital, which had a different priority and, as competition intensified throughout the international economy, were more likely to go colony-hunting with the deliberate aim of building up protected and exclusive spheres for investment, trade and sometimes, it was hoped, population transfers – though these latter were seldom very successful. The powers in question were France, Russia and, latterly, Italy and Japan.[15] So far as they achieved success their objectives were automatically in conflict with those of Britain. The aims pursued by Italy and Japan were relatively limited ones and less likely to be viewed as a serious threat. France and Russia by contrast were major powers, their colonial ambitions viewed as endangering British interests both strategically and economically in the Middle East, Africa and China. On several occasions acerbic confrontations resulted, threatening more than once to erupt into full-scale hostilities.

Leadership Contest

Neither France nor Russia, however, whatever jingoistic alarm they might evoke from time to time, was a contender for Britain's world leadership. In terms of the global economic structure they were essentially regional powers (as at that stage was the USA) however far-flung their territorial empires might be. Their war fleets and merchant fleets were far inferior to the British, their economic strength in no sense comparable. France, to be sure, was a considerable exporter of capital, but in a far more restricted fashion than Britain, indeed its principal area of foreign investment was Russia itself, its diplomatic and military ally.

The late nineteenth century saw not only the widening of the capitalist universe but its deepening and intensification as well. From the 1870s, while existing technologies were further refined and improved, a range of new ones based upon electricity, chemicals and the petrol engine were starting to make their appearance – and incidentally creating new demands for products like oil, rubber and copper, abundantly available in the territories being newly drawn into the commercial network, such as the Gulf,

Malaya or central Africa. The process is sometimes characterised as the 'second industrial revolution' and it exposed the weak side of the British economic supremacy. With these new developments Britain, in comparison to the position she already held, lagged and was deficient in innovative thrust. The reasons are complex in detail but simple enough in essence[16] – the accumulation of profitable but increasingly antiquated plant and fixed capital already *in situ*, and of course the hyper-reliance upon capital export in place of modernising investment at the productive base.

The new technologies were being exploited with far greater effect in the United States, still a world borrower rather than a lender, whose development was still bound up with its own explosively growing internal market and factors of production; and Germany, which was in a very different position altogether. With less space and fewer resources than the Americans German capital concentrated on scientific improvement, technical education and lowering unit costs. Before the end of the century it had driven British steel producers out of the markets of south eastern Europe and was challenging British manufactures in Britain itself,[17] while its expanding merchant marine did likewise on the main ocean trade routes. At the same time, though still a long way behind Britain and inferior even to France, capital exports from Germany were developing strongly. In short, Germany was emerging as a formidable competitor for Britain's position at the head of the world economic league and, with much greater modernity and efficiency both in its industrial base and banking system,[18] the likely ultimate winner.

While the nineteenth century lasted there were, apart from minor frictions over the Kaiser's sympathy for the Boer republics, no Anglo-German colonial confrontations. In fact, the German colonial empire was very small – ridiculously so in view of the country's economic and military strength – and while unofficial chauvinist groups treated this fact as a grievance, the reason was logical and straightforward enough – a formal overseas empire (except to supply bases for its expanding naval strength) was largely irrelevant to the business of German imperialism. Protectionism was not: the world as a whole with the exception of the UK was moving in a protectionist direction and this type of economic policy was vigorously practised in Germany, both for class reasons, to satisfy the agriculturally inefficient but socially powerful landed elite, and to enhance industrial strength. With the attention of German capital and the German state on world markets and world power, however, a few scraps of tropical Africa and the Pacific were of minor significance. Bismarck remarked in 1888 that his map of Africa lay in Europe.[19]

Admittedly Germany's home territory and population did not of themselves provide a sufficient base for launching the state as a world power.
The drive to subordinate foreign populations and integrate them into a
German-dominated economic framework was directed towards the east
and south, which for a continental power made a lot more sense. Well
before the end of the century the ancient Austro-Hungarian dynastic empire had been turned into an economic and diplomatic satellite. There was
no hope of replicating the British achievement with the settlement colonies as primary product suppliers and absorbers of capital, but every expectation that if the diplomatic-military arrangements could be got right
an equivalent role might be filled by the lands of the Habsburg empire and
the Balkan countries to the south east, along with Poland and the Ukraine
if they could be detached from the Russian empire. The notion of German
hegemony over eastern and south eastern Europe, accomplished through
a mixture of economic pressure and military threat – or action – was des-
ignated 'Mitteleuropa' and has been demonstrated to have operated as a
conscious long-term objective in the thinking of the German ruling class
and political/military establishment.[20] These rulers were convinced, cor-
rectly, that the German state's will to world power must ultimately be resolved by war. Their long-term but not very realistic strategy was to secure
British neutrality or neutralisation while hegemony over the continent
was attained, giving them the resources and power to tackle the British
empire itself in due course.[21]

'The most explosive version of modern imperialism', in the words of
the German historian Immanuel Geiss, was the adoption of *Weltpolitik* – a
world political stance by the German state around the turn of the century
as the new contender for world hegemony flexed its muscles.[22] The results
were initially not always too impressive,[23] but the general trend is indicative and unmistakable, and one very significant success was secured at
British expense. For many decades the politically moribund Ottoman
empire had been virtually a British satellite. As a result of developments in
the first decade of the century German diplomacy succeeded in displacing
British influence and establishing itself at Constantinople as the Turkish
regime's closest ally. German officers took over management of the Turkish army, but an even more momentous outcome was the proposal to construct a railway line from Berlin to Basra on the Gulf. The implementation
of this scheme would have enormously enhanced German commercial
influence in the Middle East and, more seriously, would bypass the Suez
Canal as the principal artery for shipping between Europe and the Far East,
with the gravest implications for the canal's value to its Anglo-French
owners. Most seriously of all it evoked the nightmare prospect of the

Kaiser's magnificent soldiers debouching on the shores of the Indian Ocean and the Gulf oilfields. Not surprisingly, the project was viewed in London (though British capital was invited to participate) with the utmost apprehension and as a major provocation on a level with the German-initiated competition in naval construction. This latter was viewed by British rulers as the unmistakable sign that the German state did indeed have the intention of eclipsing British naval supremacy and displacing Britain as the dominant global power.

The bloody contest which got underway in 1914 was therefore not so much, as Lenin phrased it, a struggle for the redivision of the world as one to determine who its leading commercial power should be; compared to which the redistribution of colonial real estate or even of spheres of trade and investment opportunity were important but secondary concerns. The line-up of opponents was altogether inevitable and the steady deterioration from the mid-1890s of the hitherto amicable Anglo-German relations was a product of the recognition by both parties that these two were destined to be the ultimate antagonists. The colonial issues which had up to that point separated Britain from France and Russia were laid aside in short order for the sake of agreements which, while they stopped short of formal military alliances, were effectively binding agreements to support each other diplomatically and in the event of war.

Combination with the two weaker of the great powers, the ones which presented no substantial threat to its global hegemony, was the natural option for the British state. The agreement in 1907 with Russia necessitated the clearing up of some still extant rivalries and suspicions, principally the question of what to do with the oil-rich Persian empire, even more moribund than its Turkish neighbour. The eventual agreement was to partition the country – the last such major act prior to the war. The Tsar was to take the north, the British the southern portion, while a section in the middle was to be very generously left to the Persians. Outstanding differences respecting frontiers in central Asia and continuing rivalries in China were likewise composed. Most symptomatically, the British empire (though in secret) pronounced its willingness to abandon a cardinal tenet of nineteenth-century British foreign policy; namely its categorical embargo upon Russian possession of Constantinople. Such a move signalled ultimate recognition by the Foreign Office and the cabinet[24] of the side upon which they knew that the diplomatic necessities of the British empire world force them to line up.

In the decade prior to 1914 a number of rehearsals took place for the general conflict that was to erupt. On these occasions the now established antagonistic blocs confronted each other, made threatening noises, per-

formed diplomatic shuffles and settled the crisis to the marginal advantage of one side or the other. Ostensibly in each case the issues at stake
were colonial or quasi-colonial ones, but should be understood rather as a
testing-out of the new alliances and manoeuvering for position. Britain's
rulers participated not so much because they instinctively wanted to than
because they felt they had no other option. Not that the British empire
was under any imaginable territorial threat: but what was most definitely
in danger from a competitor with an advantage in the technologies of the
new age was the global commercial and financial superiority of which the
empire was only the most publicly visible expression.

The Chamberlain Project

Even as these developments were in train a rival and very different notion
of what the empire should be was being promulgated in ruling class circles
and carried on to electoral platforms. The conception advanced might
possibly be termed Bismarckian – it was essentially that of the empire as a
closed and integrated economic bloc following coherent economic, political and military policies designed to match the challenge of Germany
and the USA in systematic exploitation of the most advanced technologies
and economies of scale.[25] It implied nothing less than the abandonment
of the world role hitherto played by British capital and its condensation
into an internally strengthened bloc confronting the other major blocs in
an intensified and more Darwinian struggle for world supremacy of a different sort – no longer as a global clearing house, but an aggressive competitor for privileged access to markets, resources and spheres of investment.

The prophet and promoter of this version of the imperial dream was the
Birmingham screw-manufacturer turned politician, Joseph Chamberlain.
It emerged powerfully during his period of office in Lord Salisbury's government in the 1890s and it culminated in the early years of the twentieth
century in his campaign of Tariff Reform, by which was meant the super-
session of free trade as the guiding light of commercial policy and the institution of protectionist tariffs to the disadvantage of foreign exporters
and the benefit of settlement colonies and overseas possessions.

Chamberlain aimed his appeal above all at industrial interests threatened in the British market itself, and by extension in colonial ones as well,
by cheaper foreign manufactures. Obviously he did not argue that he
wanted to perpetuate obsolescence and inefficiency in British production
methods, but rather that British industry could more readily re-equip itself and grow stronger behind tariff walls by building up the necessary

reserves for long-term investment. He canvassed working-class support in addition on the argument that protection for British industry also meant protection for jobs and, moreover, that the revenues raised from tariffs could be used to fund extensions of social welfare. 'The question is how to increase the employment of the working classes', he claimed when speaking in the East End, on the same occasion denouncing unrestricted immigration by 'aliens'. Finally, he strove to convince bankers and brokers that they too need have nothing to fear, since their profits could be maintained or even improved in a consolidated empire as readily as under the existing regime.

Chamberlain had made his initial career, in accordance with his manufacturing background appropriately enough, as a radical liberal, first as mayor of Birmingham, then as a leading figure and cabinet minister in the Liberal Party. As a proponent of modernisation he had instituted ambitious schemes of municipal reform in his home city, thereby acquiring a foundation of popular backing which he never lost during his lifetime. Partly out of frustrated egotism and partly out of genuine English nationalist convictions he led the revolt in the 1880s by a section of the Liberal Party against Gladstone's Irish policy, and from that point began to combine populist rhetoric with increasingly reactionary and imperialist stances.

His initially separate Liberal Unionist Party soon entered into effective amalgamation with the Tories, and cemented the alliance through imperial ideology. In the 1890s Chamberlain became a cabinet minister in Salisbury's administration, choosing, significantly, the Colonial Office (whose concerns did not include India). From that position Chamberlain, in a speech of 1896, advanced a scheme of imperial federation (an Imperial Federation League was already in existence, founded in 1884) designed to draw the settlement colonies closer to Britain by instituting an imperial parliamentary assembly based in London, and trade proposals intended to bind these units closer together and – although at this stage tariffs weren't mentioned – give each a bigger share in the other's trade relations.

These projects soon ran up against the realities of the British government's relationships with the settlement colonies' ruling elites. Though a Canadian premier might have agreed that 'English supremacy should last until the end of time' and the colonial (settlement colony) premiers politely attended a colonial conference in 1897 to coincide with the Diamond Jubilee, these elites were in no wise inclined to surrender their growing political autonomy, masked though it was by the deference and grovelling of Queen Victoria's Diamond Jubilee, to an imperial assembly located in London and, inevitably, dominated by the mother country. Nor

were they in any mood to see their own tender industrial growth, protected by their tariff systems, blighted by a system of imperial free trade
and free access for British producers. There did not even exist a standard
exchange rate between local colonial currencies and the pound sterling.
Chamberlain's hopes for a Federal Parliament or even a 'Council of Empire' got nowhere.

Thereafter he was occupied with more immediately pressing contingen-
cies; namely arranging the South African war and placing the Rand goldfields in politically safe hands – the successful attainment of which produced greater scope and renewed ambition to pursue the alternative
conception of empire which Chamberlain represented. In 1902 a colonial conference was organised, but the outcome was no more satisfactory
than that of 1897. Its first decision

> [r]ecognis[ed] that the principle of preferential trade between the United
> Kingdom and His Majesty's Dominions beyond the Seas would stimu-
> late and facilitate mutual commercial intercourse, and would by pro-
> moting the development of the resources and industries of the several
> parts, strengthen the Empire.

The second decision went on to flatly contradict the first, in spirit if not in
letter:

> This Conference recognises that, in the present circumstances of the
> Colonies, it is not practicable to adopt a general system of Free Trade as
> between the mother country and the British Dominions beyond the
> Seas.[26]

The following year Chamberlain resigned his government position so
as to pursue his dream more freely; he took note of past setbacks and
avoided proposals such as political federation and empire free trade with
protection against outsiders, likely to offend the settlement colony leaders, but concentrated instead on campaigning for the establishment of a
tariff wall around Britain itself, with imperial preference, which was intended to produce the same effect in the long term, without provoking
colonial antagonisms.

> I have felt for some time that this is a critical period in the history of the
> Empire. What we do now and what our colonies do will probably in
> the course of the earlier years of this century settle for all time the ques-
> tion of whether a new empire, such as has never entered into the con-

ception of man before ... whether such an empire shall be consolidated and maintained or whether we are to drop apart into several atoms, each caring only for our local and parochial interests. The Imperial idea has only recently taken root in this country ... [He goes on to reprove the colonies for lacking enthusiasm for the imperial ideal.]

But the question of trade and commerce is of the greatest importance. Unless that is satisfactorily settled, I for one do not believe in a continued union of the Empire. I hear it stated again and again by what I believe to be the representatives of a small minority of people of this country, those whom I describe, because I know no other words for them, as 'Little Englanders' – I hear it stated by them, what is a fact, that our trade with these countries is much less than our trade with foreign countries, and that therefore it appears to be their opinion that we should do everything in our power to cultivate that trade with foreigners, and that we can safely disregard the trade with our children.

That is not my conclusion. My conclusion is exactly the opposite. To look into the future, I say that it is the business of British tradesmen to do everything they can, even at some present sacrifice, to keep the trade of the colonies with Great Britain, to increase the trade and promote it, even if in doing so we lessen somewhat the trade with our foreign competitors.[27]

The concept of enhanced imperial unity supporting a more militant version of imperialism had far-reaching implications and evoked a considerable measure of support among sections of the public. It implied a more organised and disciplined population. The perils of racial degeneration were mooted and widely discussed, provoking demands for Bismarckian-style welfare initiatives. The National Service League under Field-Marshal Lord Roberts agitated for compulsory and universal military training. The Navy League, founded in 1894 to uphold British naval supremacy, had 100,000 members by 1914. Alfred Milner, former governor of South Africa, even more determined on the war than his boss Chamberlain and administratively responsible for the Chinese labour policy, emerged as a strenuous and well-connected advocate of imperial unity and authoritarian government. Juvenile organisations such the Boy Scouts, with the imperial ideology in their bloodstream, duly appeared on the scene. The Round Table was established as a kind of think-tank for the imperial elite. According to Milner:

Physical limitations alone forbid that these islands by themselves should retain the same relative importance among the vast empires of the modern world which they held in the days of smaller states – before the growth of Russia and the United States, before Germany made those giant strides in prosperity and commerce which have been the direct result of the development of her military and naval strength. These islands by themselves cannot always remain a power of the very first rank. But Greater Britain may remain such a power, humanly speaking, for ever, and by so remaining, will ensure the safety and prosperity of all the states composing it, which, again humanly speaking, nothing else can equally ensure.[28]

Yet even before these schemes of creating a closely knit imperial federation had got seriously started, the economic linchpin of the new vision, embodied in Chamberlain's Tariff Reform agenda, had been decisively broken. In the early years of the century he had succeeded in establishing a formidable coalition. A part of manufacturing industry, afflicted by foreign competition in British and international markets, was interested in the proposals. So were large sections of the landed elite and their lease-holders, severely embarrassed by the ongoing depression which had wrecked arable farming as far back as the 1870s and for whom agricultural protection would have come as a godsend. Unionist elements of the working class, above all in Chamberlain's own Birmingham constituency, were capable of being attracted as well by the prospects of increased job security and welfare.

Many millions of leaflets were distributed. Many thousands of meetings – from those on street corners to the Albert Hall – were held. The press blared daily the same message 'Tariff Reform Means Work for All'. Tariff Reform Associations were formed in hundreds of constituencies to enlist the rank-and-file behind the Chamberlain programme. Tariff reform teas were held and Tariff Reform Pagents and plays were presented. Music hall ditties were composed on the subject. Finally, the Trade Unionist Tariff Reform Association, with hundreds of local affiliates, was formed to enlist the working man to the cause ... the gramophone was used to bring Chamberlain's voice to smaller audiences; the music halls sounded to sprightly Tariff tunes ...[29]

By 1905 Chamberlain's background, reputation and demagogic energies had won over the rank and file of the Tory Party to his position. Tariff Reform with its imperialist overtones was, like unionist imperial nationalism, if not quite to the same extent, one of the hegemonic ideas which was capable of drawing together the streams of discontent upon the British right into a single current, unifying diverse class strata and assuming a populist dimension. It had geopolitical implications as well, for abandoning the pretension to perpetual global supremacy in commercial and financial transactions opened the prospect of an accommodation with Germany and agreement to divide world supremacy in those spheres instead of fighting over it – at least for the immediate future.

A Comparison

The spectacle at the opening of the twentieth century of challenge by right-wing imperialist and technocratic authoritarians to a governing liberal capitalist consensus has certain parallels with contemporary events in a country that was regarded as the weakest of the great powers, or scarcely a great power at all. If Britain had established its pre-eminent global role by the adept exploitation of *laissez-faire* principles combined with the judicious application of force where required, the ruling class in Italy had fashioned the rather rickety unity of their state by a policy of systematically bribing all interest groups capable of displaying any strength, together with a brutal form of internal colonialism, all of which meant that entrepreneurs were left with a field in which they could enrich themselves by any means that came to hand – usually corrupt and frequently violent. An empire of sorts had been acquired in Africa – principally because by then every self-respecting or aspiring power needed to have one[30] – but in the first decade of the century it was far from central to Italian realities.

In 1910 the Italian Nationalist Party (ANI), led by the journalist Corradini, was founded to promote colonial expansion, anti-parliamentarianism and economic reorganisation under the slogan of ultra-nationalism. Its spokespeople were a circle of proto-fascist intellectuals, but its backers were were the owners of the emergent high-tech industries in northern Italy, such as Fiat and Olivetti, who envied the industrial organisation, imperial successes and semi-absolute governments of Germany and Japan and dreamed of a technocratic regime willing to promote growth in the most advanced and scientific sectors of industry, discipline the labour movement and conquer new market and investment opportunities abroad. In the socio-political crisis after the war the ANI was to co-operate closely with Mussolini and eventually merge with his fascist party.

Liberal Imperialists

The Chamberlainite campaign though was all to no avail: its support, though far from negligible, was too restricted and its opponents were able to call the forces of democracy to their assistance. The new imperial idea was unable to win either at the ruling class or the popular level. So far as the former was concerned, the interests remained dominant that were committed to free trade and the functioning of the empire as an auxiliary system for a still greater role. They included still the bulk of manufacturing industry, convinced that it stood to lose more than it gained from protectionism, trading concerns of all sorts, but above all the City and the financial elite which had far too much invested, both literally and figuratively, in the existing structure to contemplate any such drastic change of direction.[31] So far as the masses were concerned, protectionism was viewed overwhelmingly in terms of agricultural tariffs, and hence of dear food, still by far the largest item of expenditure in the working-class and lower-middle-class family budget. The outcome was in 1906 the worst electoral catastrophe the Conservatives have ever experienced (not even excluding 1997), when they suffered an near wipe-out in Commons seats.[32] Ironically, the Tory leadership was not at that point advocating protection– it was the influence of Chamberlain which was feared: the leaders opposed to him were seen as hopelessly beleaguered and losing their grip on policy and control.[33] The Liberal Party inherited a stunning majority. Paradoxically, the government it formed was compelled by the imperial logic, as the German challenge advanced, not merely to retain but to strengthen and extend the imperial policy of its predecessor, along with enhanced military preparation against imperial rivals – and so to hurry the country and the empire towards the armageddon waiting for it only eight years in the future.

Further Reading

Harry Browne, *Joseph Chamberlain: Radical and Imperialist*, Longman, 1974. Short and informative.

P.J. Cain and A.G. Hopkins, *British Imperialism: Innovation and Expansion 1688–1914*, Longman, 1993.

J.M. MacKenzie, *Propaganda and Empire: The Manipulation of British Public Opinion 1880–1960*, Manchester University Press, 1984. The definitive study.

J.A. Mangan, *Making Imperial Mentalities: Socialisation and British Imperialism*, Manchester University Press, 1990. The development of imperial ideology at home and abroad.

Andrew Porter, *European Imperialism 1870–1914*, Macmillan, 1994.

Bernard Porter, *Critics of Empire: British Radical Attitudes to Colonialism in Africa 1895–1914*, Macmillan, 1968.

Edward Said, *Orientalism*, Routledge and Kegan Paul, 1978. An in-depth critique of western attitudes.

G.R. Searle, *The Quest for National Efficiency: A Study in British Politics and Political*

Thought, 1899–1914, Blackwell, 1971. The corruption of British politics and social attitudes by imperial ideology.

Bernard Semmel, *Imperialism and Social Reform: English Social-Imperial Thought 1895–1914*, Allen and Unwin, 1960. The first and very comprehensive discussion of the British version, clearly bringing out the connections between social authoritarianism in Britain and empire abroad.

A.J. Stockwell (ed.),*Cambridge Illustrated History of the British Empire*, Cambridge University Press, 1996.

R.A. Webster, *Industrial Imperialism in Italy 1908–1915*, University of California Press, 1975. Comparison with a weaker imperialism.

Martin J. Weiner, *English Culture and the Decline of the Industrial Spirit 1850–1980*, Penguin, 1985. Controversial interpretation of the relationship between empire, culture and economic decline.

6
Significance of Empire

Imperialism, as a raucously proclaimed doctrine and practice, was the most pertinent reality of British society and politics for around thirty years prior to 1914. Emerging out of a system of world commodity exchange to which British capital was centrally important it developed to supplement, reinforce and undergird that system, but not to replace one structure of accumulation with a fundamentally different one. It was indeed closely linked to the export of capital, though in an indirect rather than a simple and straightforward manner, but the other characteristics identified by Lenin as defining the era of imperialism – the growth of monopoly concentrations of capital and the increasing interprenetation of finance and industrial capital (not in any case very pronounced in Britain) – were secondary considerations.

The effect that imperialism, whether in the more obvious sense or the broader one of dominating the global exchange system, may have had upon British economic development is an issue which continues to be debated at great length and which it is possible here to do no more than touch upon. Critiques of imperialism from a liberal and a socialist standpoint have argued that the result was wholly adverse in that the diversion of capital resources to foreign investment and/or colonial expansion starved the home economy of funds which would have otherwise been available, hindered re-equipment and improvement of the established industries and retarded development of the new ones – not to speak of housing, health educational and other forms of social expenditure.

The counter-argument is that matters were not so simple. Capital export, along with cultural connection to or political control over sources of agricultural commodities and minerals, it is claimed, cheapened imports and so reduced both raw material and wage costs, while overseas investment did not really divert capital from indigenous industry since most of the overseas investment was financed out of the profits of previous foreign lending. The reality of the British situation as the world's clearing house, reinforced by empire, according to this argument not only made the City and its connected institutions enormously wealthy but exercised a healthy effect upon the economy as a whole. The status of British investments in the empire *per se* is a different, though evidently related, matter. The first question is whether these were more or less profitable than investment in British-centred enterprises. There is no consensus view among economic historians and the debate still rages – a lot depends in fact upon how the figures are calculated. My own view is that on the whole returns were indeed faster and higher and that this differential was the magnet which drew capital into the empire, both formal and informal. As Lenin noted, cheap land and cheap labour – either absolutely or relative to output – were the incentives that stimulated foreign investment as opposed to doing so in the metropole.

The second, much more speculative, consideration, is whether, had the economy been differently structured, i.e. had not been an imperial one, the overall rate of return upon investment in British industry and technology would have been greater than it was. The answer, though impossible to determine with any certainty, is probably not. The home economy of the time, apart from a very few specialised units, also rested upon a foundation of cheap labour, the central secret of profitability in British enterprise; and empire in its several senses made a considerable contribution to perpetuating that cheapness. Hence the turn-of-the-century economy as it then existed, but without the imperial advantages, would almost certainly have been less profitable than it was. To take hypothesis even farther and try to envisage the kind of development that might have occurred if British industrialisation had taken place in the absence of a position of global commercial and subsequently financial supremacy is driving speculation too far. Certainly contemporary critics of empire like Hobson were convinced that improving the rewards to labour instead of investing overseas would generate a bigger internal market and benefit capital as well in the long run. Lenin's retort was that while such a proposition might be true in the abstract, for capitalism to behave in such a way it would have to cease being capitalism. He was wrong, but not altogether so, for it required two world wars and unprecedented social upheaval before Hobson's hopes were partially and temporarily fulfilled.

What can be claimed with some certainty is that the character of economic, social and political structures, as they had developed out of eighteenth-century commercial supremacy and the peculiarities of the British industrialisation process as seen in both capital and labour markets, shifted emphasis and incentive away from any directed or urgent pressure towards technological updating and renovation,[1] so that even disregarding uncontrollable factors like inferior population and resources, British industry lost ground to its US and German competitors beyond what was intrinsically necessary. The defence made of late nineteenth-century British entrepreneurs is that they successfully pursued the highest returns wherever the market led them.[2] Exactly so. It was the global market structured by the dominant elite's imperial vocation which placed them in such a situation. The Chamberlainites, it may be said, were aware of the problem, and wanted to address it by means of a rigged imperial market and authoritarian social policies.

In other words the industrial economy, in terms of contemporary standards, was failing in relation to roughly equivalent economies, for reasons linked to imperialism, although no particular group of individuals can be identified as being 'to blame'. It was one case where structure unquestionably prevailed over agency. Even more unquestionably the ethos of imperialism, in its simplest sense, poisoned the cultural and intellectual atmosphere of the times, infecting every class and faction of class, producing a collective mentality that strengthened social subordination and inflamed mindless patriotism. In Semmel's words, referring to the interwar years: 'Whereas the earlier social-imperialists had spoken *sotto voce*, Mosley shouted, but the elements of his doctrine were the same as theirs.'[3]

The exotic aspects of empire were admirably fitted for spectacle and display. A propaganda barrage running the gamut from sermons and tabloid journalism through scientific and academic texts to colonial exhibitions and Empire Day inculcated recognition of the empire as a fact of nature destined to last a thousand years – at least. It sustained and conferred status upon a military caste which British civic culture and government parsimony would not have tolerated if based permanently in the home islands. It provided the opportunity for scions of the aristocracy and *haute bourgeoisie* to lord it over pigmented populations with less restraint than they had to show towards enfranchised members of the British lower classes,[4] and in doing so fostered in them attitudes which they reimported to the home country, reinforcing their presumption of governing it too by divine right. It was a presumption which rubbed off upon sections of the lower orders as well. The deference vote, reinforced by the jingoism which imperialism inflated to yet wider dimensions, had always been present since the arrival of a mass electorate and was assiduously cultivated by Disraeli in the first instance. Did not the feat of governing a quarter of the world's population in the face of jealous rivals demonstrate beyond the last scintilla of doubt that the upper classes indeed possessed the qualities which entitled them to command the lesser breeds at home as well as abroad?

Evidence of racial superiority was proferred to even the lowliest Briton (all too often with gratifying success) by reminding him (or less frequently her) that the nation he belonged to ruled over the mightiest empire in history and he was part of the achievement. More concretely, racism was propagated at a mass level by emigrants who settled in South Africa or Kenya or the rank and file British soldiers who served in the Indian army. In both cases their experience of relations with conquered colonial populations was such as to make racist assumptions second nature. Overall, these may not have constituted an enormous number of individuals, but they all had families and circles of friends with whom they were in communication and who absorbed their experience at second hand. In short, the ideology of empire put down deep, deep roots into British society and its collective consciousness.

It penetrated even the contemporary labour movement. 'Few members of the British working class evidently saw subjects of the empire as fellow victims with whom they should identify.'[5] Lenin, writing in 1916 when he had particular reasons for postulating such a relationship, blamed the corruption on 'labour lieutenants of capital' – MPs, party functionaries, trade union officers, who were allegedly bribed out of the superprofits generated from imperialism, as an insurance policy on the part of capital, and who were responsible (he did not have only Britain in mind) for blinding, misleading and politically enervating the mass of workers whose class instincts remained sound and who themselves gained no benefit from the existence of imperialism. When capital could no longer afford such bribery, Lenin declared, the proletariat would be in a position to understand the true situation.

The picture is overly simplistic. The stratum of full-time labour leaders that the workers' movements had brought into existence had indeed long ceased to have a revolutionary consciousness, if they ever did, but Lenin's strictures and attributions of motive are much too crude and unhistorical. The 'labour lieutenants' succumbed to the imperial embrace not as a rule because their palms were crossed with silver exacted from imperial superprofits but because imperialism was the climate of the times and there appeared to be, in the words of a later reactionary, 'no alternative'.

The framework of assumptions which the trade union movement and the nascent Labour Party brought to their perspectives on the empire in the early years of the century therefore accepted its permanence and the duty of British governments and administrators to guide and direct the fortunes of communities standing at what, it was taken for granted, was a lower level of civilisation – even if the movement's spokespeople proposed to guide and direct them in a generally more humane manner than the ruling class had been accustomed to do. 'Hence it came about that while they day-dreamed of transforming the empire into a true federation, in reality the empire was transforming them. They were soon growing content to change it by giving it a new look, contemplating it in a new light, as Hegel did with Prussian autocracy.'[6] The Webbs in 1902 formed a dining club, called the Coefficients, with the purpose of promoting among the political elite the notions of national efficiency and a strong empire, and the Director of their intellectual offspring, the London School of Economics, was W. A. S. Hewins, a rabid imperialist.[7]

To some extent this was a question of self-interest as well as humanitarian impulse. Labour leaders were conscious of the dangers of wages in Britain being undercut by cheap colonial labour employed in enterprises paying subsistence wages or less and wholly lacking in labour protection or control. The textile mills beginning to appear in India were an immediate and pertinent instance. British labour was to the fore in the campaign against 'Chinese slavery' in South Africa which contributed to the epic Conservative defeat of 1906, and we have already noted George Bernard Shaw's reaction to the Denshawni horror. So far as the political aspirations of colonial populations were concerned, however, the official labour movement scarcely improved upon the hostility and incomprehension emanating from bourgeois sources. 'We have a diverting picture of Keir Hardie,' writes Victor Kiernan, '(... the man who had staggered Westminster by turning up at the House in a cloth cap, as if bent on immediate red revolution) gravely conversing with a magistrate in Benares on the importance of encouraging landowners and others with a stake in the country, as a moderating influence.'[8] Bernard Semmel lists around a dozen trade unionists in leading positions who were associated with Chamberlain's Tariff Reform campaign.[9]

Turning to the intellectual or revolutionary wings of the movement does not present a radically more encouraging picture. The Fabian Society, which saw socialism being attained in the long run via reformist bureaucratic efficiency, was in fact the most articulate exponent of labour imperialism and envisaged the empire with its human and material resources as an integral part of an advance to socialism for the British people – almost a left-wing equivalent of Chamberlainism. 'Theoretically [the Rand] should be internationalised, not British-Imperialised; but until the Federation of the world becomes an accomplished fact, we must accept the most responsible Imperial federations available as a substitute for it', wrote Bernard Shaw in *Fabianism and the Empire.* 'The design of socialism in this pattern is to turn Empires into true Commonwealths. Shaw's manifesto imagines a Fabianising of the Empire in the cause of efficiency – a cause that Webb himself was to put his signature to the following year with Tract No. 108, *A Policy of National Efficiency.'*[10] At the other end of the socialist spectrum in Britain the Social Democratic Federation, with Marxism as its formal ideology, was led by H. M. Hyndman, an avowed and unashamed imperialist and strenuous advocate of a big navy on social-imperialist grounds – i.e. not only would it consolidate the empire and deter foreigners but also provide employment in British ship yards. Possibly 'the left never wavered in its condemnation of colonial wars and conquests'[11] but it did not seriously challenge the existence of empire. At best 'their analysis and definitions of the new "imperialist" phase of capitalism ... rightly saw colonial annexation and exploitation simply as one symptom and characteristic of that new phase: undesirable like all its characteristics, but not in itself central'.[12]

Opponents

For an opponent of empire on principle it was a depressing spectacle, and there were some who managed to rise above the horizon of imperialist presumptions. Two individuals who were themselves part of the elite and notable for their careers in exposing imperialist atrocity were Wilfrid Scawen Blunt and Roger Casement. The former denounced imperialism in the Middle East and the manoeuvres and violence by which its territories had been brought under British control. The latter, as a British consul, publicised the horrors of rubber extortion in South America and King Leopold's Congo. These, of course, were not British colonies and indeed Casement was awarded a knighthood by HM government in recognition of his humanitarian endeavours. His turning against British imperialism led him to identify with the movement for Irish independence and led him to execution in 1916 for a different kind of anti-imperialist endeavour. As opponents of and propagandists against particular abuses of empire E. D. Morel should be mentioned, as should the Aborigines' Protection Society, although the latter, understandably enough in the circumstances, often favoured direct government control with London-appointed officials as a check on the depredations of settlers and freebooters.

One British name stands out as a critic who generalised from the particular circumstances of South Africa to launch a thoroughgoing critique of imperialism as an economic reality and mainstay of political culture. This was J. A. Hobson, who in politics was a Liberal. In *Imperialism* (1902)

Hobson interpreted the expansionism of the previous twenty years as an effect of capital seeking new fields of investment abroad – which he defined as 'the economic taproot of imperialism' – in consequence of restricted markets at home, the restriction itself being attributed to deficiency of demand arising from the low incomes suffered by the majority of the population. Hobson condemned imperialism as detrimental to Britain's economy and society in a number of dimensions. By diverting capital abroad it did more than simply retard the improvement and expansion of the country's industrial base, it centred economic (and ultimately political) power in the financial elite and their hangers-on concentrated in south-east England, and threatened ultimately the fate of deindustrialisation.

Hobson recommended as an alternative to imperialism a deliberate programme of increasing consuming power among the masses through enhanced wages and welfare benefits – a sort of proto-Keynsianism. Lenin, when he came to write *Imperialism: The Highest Stage of Capitalism* esteemed Hobson's analysis very highly, above that of German Social Democrat commentators, to the degree that historians have referred – inaccurately – to the Hobson–Lenin thesis. In fact, Lenin wholly rejected an important aspect of Hobson's argument, namely the underconsumptionist thesis which attributed the pressure to invest abroad to deficiency of home demand. 'The profits are higher – that is all' was Lenin's alternative,[13] and as noted above he regarded Hobson's ideas of increasing workers' consuming power as wholly utopian.

It has to be acknowledged that in spite of the the work and writing of these as well as less celebrated individuals, prior to 1914 there was no collective and organised opposition to imperialism in Britain and the the ripple of public disquiet and reaction which followed the indifferent performance of British arms in the South African war, together with revelations of how concentration camps had been used to grind down the Boer resistance, did not fundamentally affect the picture. Following World War I, however, even as the empire set its bounds still wider, popular imperialism had become what Americans would call a busted flush: the experience of that war, Irish revolt, Russian revolution and events in India had soured public attitudes irrevocably to the myths and pretences that had formerly sustained the imperial dream. The earlier anti-imperial voices crying in the wilderness now resonated with the disillusion felt towards the entire economic and political system which had produced first the holocaust of the trenches and then in the immediate aftermath economic collapse and immiseration. Colonial liberation, if it still had a very considerable distance and another world war to go, was now at least thinkable.

That, however, remained a minority trend for the time being. Perhaps the most remarkable political fact of the interwar years is that with the most democratic franchise yet seen the Conservatives, the party of unregulated markets, imperial flag-waving and nostalgia, easily dominated the electoral history of those decades. Nevertheless, when compared with the prewar ecstasies, even the Tories' enthusiasm appeared half-hearted and lacking in conviction, and the protected trading bloc brought into existence after 1932 following the abandonment of the gold standard was nothing more than a parodic caricature of Chamberlain's grand Imperial Federation.

These developments regrettably did not represent a final abandonment of imperial megalomania. World War II, while it produced enormously positive effects in British social relations and politics, also to an extent revived imperial sentiment, since as part of the life-and-death combat against fascism, the empire, along with other outmoded and baneful institutions, could be presented in a comparatively favourable and rejuvenated light, and as we now know it totally seduced the ministers of Attlee's 1945–51 government.[14] Overseas possessions were only a part of this vision – indeed the lesser part – and India was surrendered with relative equanimity and goodwill: the objective was to continue to play the role of a Great Power, both financially and militarily, only this time under the umbrellas of the US dollar in the first instance and US nuclear armoury in the second.

These twin aims have constituted the maleficent heritage of imperialism which fatally undermined the social programme and the electoral viability of Attlee's governments. They continued to form the central purpose of his successors and lie at the root of the dramatic failure of the British economy during the second half of the twentieth century. The life-draining ambition to cut a major figure on the world financial stage remains in place and continues to devastate what remains of the country's industrial capacity as well as its social infrastructures, for though the form would change with European monetary integration, the reality would not. Even the apparently buried memory of worldwide possessions and military power exercised across the globe is capable of dramatic resurgence with momentous political results, as the Falklands War demonstrated only too forcefully. The spectre of empire continues to stalk Britain, and on the eve of the twenty-first century it has still to be exorcised. The history of the modern world has been structured by imperialism, with the events of the years 1870–1914 constituting only one stage in a process which is still ongoing. All nations have been profoundly affected by it, but none more so than Britain, the most successful practitioner of overseas colonialism. The empire on which the sun never set is still casting its shadow.

Notes

Preface

1. Andrew Porter, *European Imperialism 1860–1914*, Macmillan, 1994, p.39.
2. See especially Victor Kiernan, *Marxism and Imperialism*, Edward Arnold, 1974, pp.37–60.
3. It is worth noting that Hitler intensely admired the British achievement in conquering and ruling India and that his favourite film was *Bengal Lancer*.
4. For example, George Bernard Shaw on the Denshawni Horror of 1906 – see below.

Introduction

1. Malcolm Bradbury, *The Modern World: Ten Great Writers*, Penguin, 1989, p.85.
2. Ibid., p.256.
3. Ibid., p.277.
4. A.J. Stockwell (ed.), *Cambridge Illustrated History of the British Empire*, Cambridge University Press, 1996, p.168.
5. Robert Bartlett, *The Making of Europe*, Penguin, 1993, pp.313–14.
6. Michael Hechter, *Internal Colonialism*, Routledge and Kegan Paul, 1975. The north-east of Ireland also saw (in the seventeenth century) colonisation in the modern sense – the displacement of the native Irish by settlers from mainland Scotland.
7. The bullion came partly from plunder and partly from slave-worked mines. Its importance came from its role as the basis for liquid capital: its inflationary impact has been exaggerated.
8. Or 'gentlemanly capitalists', the phrase of P.J. Cain and A.G. Hopkins, *British Imperialism: Innovation and Expansion 1688–1914*, Longman, 1993.
9. By the Treaty of Utrecht in 1713, following the Anglo-Scottish state's first major commercial war, British merchants acquired the monopoly of supplying slaves to the Iberian colonies of South America.
10. The concept of 'Industrial Revolution' has attracted nearly as much debate as the question of imperialism. I am treating it as a self-evident reality.
11. Although there was one important exception: the loss of the American tobacco monopoly by Glasgow merchants stimulated industrial development in that region.
12. *Capital*, vol. 1, Penguin edition, 1976, p.926.
13. This concept was initially advanced by Emannuel Arrighi in *The Long Twentieth Century*, Verso, 1994, though his interpretation differs from mine in certain respects.
14. There were yet further British territorial acquisitions after 1918, with the share-out of spoils from the defeated German and Turkish empires, but by then the political imperial structure had entered irreversible decline. See John Callaghan's *Great Power Complex: British Imperialism, International Crises and National Decline, 1914–51*, Pluto Press, 1997.
15. But see the arguments advanced by Perry Anderson at various points, com-

mencing with 'Origins of the Present Crisis', *New Left Review* 23, Jan./Feb. 1964. These writers stress the social and political weight of a commercial and financial bourgeoisie linked to landed wealth.

16. P.J. Marshall, 'The World Shaped by Empire', in Stockwell (ed.), *Cambridge Illustrated History of the British Empire*, p.10.

17. Not only the Bengal weavers suffered in this episode. The Indian export trade provided the necessary foundation for the expansion of mechanised weaving in Britain which destroyed the British handloom weaving industry, along with most of its workforce.

18. E.E. Williams' alarmist tract published by Heinemann in 1896 (reprinted Harvester 1973) under the title *Made in Germany* warned the British public that the very internal markets of the UK were being colonised by German products.

19. The two most notorious instances were the production of aniline dyestuffs and 'basic' steel where British inventions had been exploited in Germany to create new industries.

20. Also studies of imperialism written in the years before World War 1, by J.A. Hobson (from whom Lenin derived much of his information in relation to the British variety), Rudolf Hildfering, Rosa Luxemburg and Nikolai Bukharin.

21. V.I. Lenin, *Selected Works*, Vol. 5, Lawrence & Wishart, 1936, p.31.

22. See the first two chapters of Kiernan, *Marxism and Imperialism*, for a discussion of these relations.

Chapter 1. The British Empire on the Eve

1. The circumstances of the period of late nineteenth-century empire building might well have reversed the terms and been called 'the free trade of imperialism'.

2. *The Communist Manifesto*, intro. Eric Hobsbawm, Verso, 1998, pp.39–40.

3. With the development of refrigeration in the 1880s even certain perishable products, mainly carcasses, could be incorporated into long-distance trade.

4. The slowing pace of railway construction in Britain during the second half of the century made it more important for railway contractors to find markets abroad, particularly in India and the settlement colonies.

5. The British government was seriously considering withdrawal from its West African outposts.

6. Not everywhere however. The influential German economic thinker Frederick List argued for the importance of protection in developing 'infant industries'.

7. Quoted in E.L. Woodward, *The Age of Reform*, Oxford, 1938, p.412.

8. Cain and Hopkins, *British Imperialism*, pp.329–30.

9. In some cases, such as China and the Ottoman empire, the semi-colony status was imposed by several European powers acting conjointly. This had been the original intended form of control for Egypt as well, but in the end that became a virtual colony of Britain alone.

10. Edward Thompson, 'The Peculiarities of the English', *Socialist Register*, 1965, p.343.

11. The practice of transporting involuntary ones – convicts to Tasmania and Australia – ceased in the 1850s.

12. Sometimes also a mineral potential, as with Australian gold.

13. '... what "maturity" meant to the British, among other things, was that some of the colonies in Canada and Australia had developed into well-ordered capitalist societies capable of functioning as satellite economies without direct intervention', Cain and Hopkins, *British Imperialism*, p. 238.
14. An intriguing sidelight upon this is that the cattle ranching enterprises of the south-western states, the material foundation for the cultural artefact of the wild west, were largely funded from Dundee.
15. In the words of one Viceroy, Lord Mayo, 'We are all British gentlemen engaged in the magnificent work of governing an inferior race', C.C. Eldridge, *Victorian Imperialism*, Hodder & Stoughton, 1978, p.223. 'A despotism controlled from home' according to the first Secretary of State for India, ibid., p.224.
16. Stockwell (ed.), *Cambridge Illustrated History of the British Empire*, p.156.
17. Indentured workers were brought from India to British Guiana as a more reliable labour force than the former slaves were thought to be.
18. 'Niggers are tigers', was the remark of the poet laureate, Alfred, Lord Tennyson, quoted in Porter, *European Imperialism*, p.24.
19. Though the Irish Home Rule MPs elected under the new franchise most certainly did.
20. 'One nation' was the slogan which encapsulated this approach.
21. Seeley's *Expansion of England*, published in 1883 and a runaway success, was based on lecture courses prepared in the 1870s.
22. See Tom Nairn, *The Enchanted Glass: Britain and its Monarchy*, Radius, 1988.

Chapter 2. The Drive into Africa

1. In the 1830s the ruler of Egypt, Mehemet Ali, acted in complete independence of his nominal sovereign, waged war against him and even came close to capturing Constantinople until prevented by the British, who did not want Middle East power relations disturbed to their potential disadvantage.
2. E. J. Hobsbawm, *The Age of Empire 1875–1914*, Weidenfeld & Nicolson, 1987, p.74
3. L.C.B. Seaman, *Victorian England*, Routledge, 1993, p.357.
4. Its leader, Arabi Pasha, was deported rather than being handed over for execution – perhaps a sign of bad conscience on the part of Gladstone's government.
5. 'The assertion that the British government did not desire to occupy Egypt only amounts to saying that it would have preferred to go on with the cheaper method of letting Egypt be exploited through a native puppet; just as the US marines are only sent to a banana-republic when the local dictator fails to deliver the bananas', Kiernan, *Marxism and Imperialism*, p.77.
6. Some newspapers reporting Gordon's death were printed with special black borders.
7. *The Times*, editorial, 3 May 1884.
8. R. Robinson and J. Gallagher in their celebrated *Africa and the Victorians*, Macmillan, 1961, use this fact as evidence that African affairs were regarded by British governments mostly as an irritating sideline with no economic implications, and the partition determined purely by determination to protect the sea-routes to India.
9. Shortly thereafter a British agent was put in place as the Sultan's first minister.

10. The agreement arrived at with Germany involved the transfer of the island of Heligoland, a British dependency off the coast of Germany, to German sovereignty – in spite of the unwillingness and protests of the Heligolanders. The episode makes an interesting comparison with the Falklands affair in 1982.
11. The large, ethnically mixed population of 'Coloureds' should also be noted.
12. See Charles van Onselen, 'Randlords and Rotgut', *History Workshop* 2, 1976.
13. Not that Rhodes remained content with such modest ambitions. His will – *in 1873* – provided for the funding of a secret society with the objective of extending British rule around the globe and directly occupying,'the entire continent of Africa, the Holy Land, the valley of the Euphrates, the islands of Cyprus and Candia, the whole of South America, the islands of the Pacific not heretofore possessed by great Britain, the whole of the Malay archipelago, the sea-board of China and Japan, the ultimate recovery of the United States as an integral part of the British Empire ...' – making the contemporaneous perspectives of Bartle Frere appear modest indeed.
14. 'In securing this privilege Rhodes was greatly assisted by Sir Hercules Robinson, the Governor of the Cape, who had sizeable investments in Rhodes companies and was economical with the truth in presenting the Company's credentials', Cain and Hopkins, *British Imperialism*, p.376.
15. M.E. Chamberlain, *The Scramble for Africa*, Longman, 1974, pp.135–6.
16. *London Gazette*, 13 July 1886.
17. It is an interesting aside to note the assumption that the concepts of English property law could be directly applied to the populations of the African savannah belt.
18. Evidently this clause was varied for Muslim rulers who were literate in Arabic.
19. The analyses of Fritz Fischer are crucial for understanding, from the German angle, the links between imperialism and the origins of World War I. See his *Germany's Aims in the First World War*, Chatto and Windus, 1967.
20. Kiernan, *Marxism and Imperialism*, p.79.

Chapter 3. Other Extensions

1. Cain and Hopkins, *British Imperialism*, p.335.
2. Ibid., p.338.
3. Ibid., p.342.
4. Ibid., p.341.
5. Ibid., p.350.
6. The drug was also extensively used in Britain, famously by artists and literatii, but also generally as an analgesic – all that was available prior to aspirin – and even as a pacifier for babies.
7. Cain and Hopkins, *British Imperialism*, pp.425–6.
8. Quoted in ibid., p.429.
9. The under-secretary at the Foreign Office was a substantial shareholder.
10. Which, incidentally, did much to increase British business with Japan as well.
11. Where, interestingly, they continued to maintain a nominal 'emperor'.
12. A *Punch* cartoon of 1898 shows John Bull trying to restrain a Frenchman, German and Russian from tearing apart a helpless emperor.
13. An interesting comparison suggests itself with Tsarist Russia, where in 1905–6,

to protect the already enormous French stake in the country, the French government and investors intervened with a loan to save the regime from being swept away by revolution.

14. Cain and Hopkins, *British Imperialism*, p.441.
15. One such suitable authority was the compliant Siamese monarchy. Consequently that state escaped formal annexation.
16. 'In 1896 reinforcements enabled a large-scale "pacification"(the favourite European term) to be undertaken, [in northern Sumatra] and in the next few years the Dutch – whose long-lost kinsmen in South Africa were just being pacified by the British – broke the back of the resistance', V.G. Kiernan, *European Empires from Conquest to Collapse*, Fontana, 1982, pp.108.
17. According to R.C.K. Ensor, 'perhaps the most successful of her tropical colonies', *England 1870–1914*, Oxford, 1936.
18. L.L. Gardiner and J.H. Davidson, *British Imperialism in the late 19th Century*, Edward Arnold, 1968, pp.46–7.
19. It was, of course, in its origins a counter-revolutionary war, but with the establishment of the Napoleonic imperial regime that aspect had become a secondary one.
20. Cain and Hopkins, *British Imperialism*, p.301.
21. British public opinion, however, was divided over whether the Ottoman regime deserved to be propped up. Its tendency from time to time to massacre its Christian subjects constituted extremely bad public relations.
22. In 1914 it had about 700 offices and 9,000 employees. 'It virtually controlled central government finance, exerted great influence over railway concessions and other developmental projects and received diplomatic support from the major powers and assistance from the principal foreign banks', Cain and Hopkins, *British Imperialism*, p.405.
23. Ironically, the two worst defeats suffered by British (and imperial) forces during the war were inflicted by the Turks – at Gallipoli and the lesser-known surrender at Kut in Mesopotamia.
24. See below, Chapter 5.
25. The point applies with equal force to Afghanistan, which greatly exercised the Foreign and India Offices (to the extent that a declaration of war against Russia was actually printed in the 1880s), but where few could have hoped for significant returns on investment – least of all on loans to rulers.

Chapter 4. The Evolved Imperial Structure

1. And some not very developed ones, such as the Russian empire.
2. But see below, Chapter 5.
3. At least outside the island of Tasmania, where the indigenous population was actually exterminated – the only example of total genocide in nineteenth-century colonisation.
4. Ensor, *England 1870–1914*, p.377.
5. A tropical fruit, the banana, introduced to British tables in the 1870s, gave an enhanced importance to the West Indian colonies.
6. The usual methods of meeting the government debt payments were by taxes on agriculture exports and imports. The peasant producers paid, by being com-

pelled to export any surplus above subsistence (and frequently were driven into destitution or starvation) and by paying a higher price for imported commodities they might use.

7. Egypt being a particular case in point.
8. Investments were made for instance in Bihari coal mines. By the early twentieth century factory textile production was of growing significance.
9. The ferocity of King Leopold's regime in the Congo Free State was the product not purely of sadism on the part of his officials and African allies, but also of the intrinsic difficulty of establishing routine systems of exploitation in the conditions of the equatorial rain forest.
10. A. Keppel-Jones, *South Africa: A Short History*, Hutchinson, 1961, p.175. These contract labourers were recruited on comparatively generous terms, being given land grants at the end of their contract. Some wealthier Indians also arrived spontaneously to take advantage of commercial opportunities.
11. The practice of indentured labour had started well before the era of late nineteenth-century imperialism – indeed, as soon as slavery was abolished in the British empire. The first Indian indentured labourers were shipped to Mauritius in 1834.
12. Though not always, when bigger issues were at stake. French officials seized without compensation the property of a British trader on the West African island of Matacong. Despite intensive lobbying Lord Salisbury's government refused to react, because such intervention would have detracted from the success of a satisfactory border agreement.
13. The famous verse about the Maxim gun tells its own story. The case of the dum-dum bullet is also relevant. The expanding bullet was so named because of its production in the Indian cantonment of Dum Dum. It was devised specifically because it was asserted that regular bullets were incapable of stopping 'savages'.
14. In 1881 69,647 British troops were stationed in India, with 125,000 Indians serving in the British army. The next largest colonial garrison was positioned in Malta – its strength was 5,626, Porter, *European Imperialism*. By 1906 the figures were respectively 74,000 and 157,000, together with around 100,000 reserves and auxiliaries and 146,000 troops from the Indian princely states.
15. Russia was in fact regarded as Britan's most serious imperial rival, the interests which it was felt to threaten being far more important than any menaced by French expansion in Africa.
16. The prohibition, R. Palme Dutt remarks, was applauded by progressive Indian opinion of the time, *India Today*, Gollancz, 1940, p.273.
17. The earlier abolition of slavery, by the Jacobin-dominated Convention in France in 1793, was of course quietly forgotten.
18. The Trinidadian writer and historian, Eric Williams, had claimed in *Capitalism and Slavery* (University of North Carolina Press, 1944) that the slave trade's profits were the foundation of the Industrial Revolution, but this probably exaggerates the relationship, although it was certainly important.
19. The more famous producers of boys' fiction on imperial themes were skilled and able story-tellers, as I can testify from personal experience; names such as Rider Haggard and G.A. Henty.
20. Journals such as the *Illustrated London News*, through the medium of engravings, provided visual commentary.

21. One popular Sunday newspaper was even entitled *Empire News*.
22. Kipling was more than a vulgar imperial publicist (though he was certainly that as well): he shows a keen appreciation of many of the contradictions involved in exercising imperial authority on the ground.
23. I have been unable to locate the author or poem's title, but the memory is a vivid one from my schooldays.
24. The term itself was more commonly used by the French, but the concept was general among the imperial powers.
25. In this his proposal was largely supported by advanced Indian opinion. As a historian Macauley showed little interest in the empire.
26. They were answered, however, by a variety of progressive and liberal opinion, notably John Stuart Mill. See, for example, John Saville and E.P. Thompson, 'John Stuart Mill and EOKA', *New Reasoner* 7, Winter 1958–59.
27. David Fieldhouse, 'For Richer, for Poorer?' in Stockwell (ed.), *Cambridge Illustrated History of the British Empire*, p.124.
28. In his State of the Union Address of 1870 President Grant looked forward with enthusiasm to the total extirpation of the American Indians. Another US President, Theodore Roosevelt, was to declare that a war against savages was the most justified of all wars.
29. The leading Scottish daily papers, the *Scotsman* and *Glasgow Herald*, for example, switched their politics from Liberal to Conservative.
30. A development assisted by the fact that no firearms restrictions existed before 1920.

Chapter 5. Imperial Relations

1. In absolute numbers, however, the figures are less impressive. Between 1876 and 1914 Canada received 1.5 million British immigrants, Australia and New Zealand between them 800,000 and South Africa 136,000.
2. Particularly in relation to colonial tariffs – see below.
3. A.J. Stockwell comments on the contrast between the modest official residence of the British prime minister and the intimidating magnificence of government houses anywhere in the dependent empire, *Cambridge Illustrated History of the British Empire*, p.166.
4. Tapan Raychaudhuri, 'British Rule in India: An Assessment, in Stockwell (ed.), *Cambridge Illustrated History of the British Empire*, p.360.
5. At the end of the twentieth century it is hard to appreciate how sensational and *revolutionary* such a demand sounded at the time.
6. The question arises naturally as to why the European conquistadores bothered with such 'treaties'. This perfunctory legalism, however, was essential to avert possible objections in the home country to their activities and also as a bargaining counter in relation to European rivals.
7. Stockwell, 'Power, Authority and Freedom', in Stockwell (ed.), *Cambridge Illustrated History of the British Empire*, p.163.
8. The otherwise unimpressive colony of Aden had the inestimable merit of controlling the southern entrance to the Red Sea, as British-occupied Egypt did its north.
9. See V.G. Kiernan, 'Empires and Umpires', *Socialist History* 13, November 1998, pp.1–4.

10. The trend towards the growth during this period of huge monopoly concerns and cartels was most marked in the USA and Germany; much less so in Britain, though it was present there as well. The cartels might well cross national boundaries, as with the French and German steel industries, or, most notoriously, the shipping conferences, which kept a tight grip on the international carrying trade.
11. The nearest example was undoubtedly the USA.
12. For example, French peasants or Prussian Junkers.
13. The British government, however, borrowed heavily from the USA to finance the Boer War, the first example of it undertaking extensive borrowing abroad. It was an early sign of what was to become a central relationship in the later twentieth century.
14. Though Malaya and the Middle East did become centrally important on account of their raw material output.
15. Those listed had pretensions to great power status. Portugal, though it had an extensive colonial empire, did not.
16. See, for example, P.L. Payne, *British Entrepreneurship in the Nineteenth Century*, Macmillan, 1974; Martin J. Weiner, *English Culture and the Decline of the Industrial Spirit 1850–1980*, Penguin, 1985.
17. Williams, *Made in Germany*.
18. The German banking cartels were directly involved in industrial investment to a much greater extent than those of other states.
19. Porter, *European Imperialism*, p.17.
20. See Fritz Fischer, *Germany's Aims in the First World War*.
21. The German strategists reckoned, however, that if continental control could be secured, a direct confrontation with Britain itself might be made unnecessary.
22. This is not to ignore the fact that the German elite was itself internally divided on the issue of world strategy and subject to conflicting pressures from patriotic mass organisations. See Geoff Eley, '*Sammlungspolitik*, Social Imperialism and the Navy Law of 1898', in his *From Unification to Nazism: Reinterpreting the German Past*, Allen & Unwin, 1986.
23. For example, aggressive naval postures in Morocco and Venezuela and the provocative (to the UK) naval expansion which the Reich undertook.
24. Not all cabinet members were admitted to the secret.
25. A publication by this lobby, C.S. Goldman (ed.), *The Empire and the Century*, Charles Murray, 1906, speculates on the likelihood of the USA, Russia and the British empire becoming the three world powers of the twentieth century – or the danger of the USA alone becoming hegemonic, even over the UK; J.L. Garvin, 'The Maintenance of Empire', in ibid., pp.69–143.
26. Quoted in Harry Browne, *Joseph Chamberlain: Radical and Imperialist*, Longman, 1974, pp.92–3.
27. Speeches in March and May 1903. Ibid pp. 94–6.
28. Quoted in P.J. Marshall, '1870–1918: The Empire under Threat', in Stockwell (ed.), *Cambridge Illustrated History of the British Empire*, p.59.
29. Bernard Semmel, *Imperialism and Social Reform: English Social-Imperial Thought 1895–1914*, Allen & Unwin, 1960, pp.110–11.
30. In 1896 an Italian army was annihilated by the Ethiopians at Adowa, frustrating the attempt to make that country into an Italian colony. This worst defeat ever suffered by Europeans in an African conflict was made possible by

the supply of French armaments to the Ethiopians.

31. Cain and Hopkins note the irony that if the Chamberlainite campaign had succeeded and Britain's manufactured exports become more competitive it could have damaged London's position at the centre of the international economy by forcing competitors who were also borrowers to reduce their prices, accept lower profit margins, and thereby impair the ability to repay their debts, *British Imperialism*, p.314.

32. The figure was 157 seats on the former government side, to 513 for the Liberal coalition. The prime minister, Arthur Balfour, lost his own seat.

33. The Conservative Party conference had voted with Chamberlain. Balfour commented that he would sooner take advice from his valet than from a Conservative Conference. An empire trading bloc was eventually constructed in 1932, but by then it was much too late to have any meaning in respect of Chamberlain's hopes.

Chapter 6. Significance of Empire

1. Reflected also in the fact that the most innovative and export-successful sector of British industry has been armaments production.

2. The case for the entrepreneurs' defence can be summarised as follows: '... when one attempts to understand the specific problems that were being encountered by industrial firms ... one can seldom fault the solution arrived at in the light of the available information at the disposal of the entrepreneur or the board at the time of the decision'. P.L. Payne, *British Entrepreneurship in the Nineteenth Century*, Macmillan, 1974, p.58.

3. Semmel, *Imperialism and Social Reform*, p.251.

4. Indicative is the notorious remark by Lord Curzon (who was actually by the standards of imperial administrators a comparatively humane ruler), upon seeing some British soldiers bathing, that he had not appreciated that the lower classes had such white skins.

5. P.J. Marshall, 'Imperial Britain', in Stockwell (ed.), *Cambridge Illustrated History of the British Empire*, p.321.

6. Kiernan, *Marxism and Imperialism*, p.238.

7. Semmel, *Marxism and Social Reform*, p.170. Semmel comments, 'Milner's "nobler Socialism" was in conception little different from the "collectivism" of the Fabians who considered the South African consul most worthy of their praise.'

8. Kiernan, *Marxism and Imperialism*, p.247.

9. Semmel, *Marxism and Social Reform*, pp.114–15.

10. Michael Holroyd, *Bernard Shaw*, vol. 2, *The Pursuit of Power*, Random House, New York, 1989, p.44.

11. E. J. Hobsbawm, *The Age of Empire 1875–1914*, p.72.

12. Ibid.

13. Kiernan, *Marxism and Imperialism*, p.43.

14. 'After World War II, when Whitehall designed a new era of colonial rule, Britain aimed to reposition the empire in the Middle East and Africa'. Cain and Hopkins, *British Imperialism*, p.421.

Select Bibliography

Adelman, Paul, *Gladstone, Disraeli and Later Victorian Politics*, Longman, 1970.
Anderson, Perry, 'Origins of the Present Crisis' *New Left Review* 23, Jan./Feb. 1964.
Arrighi, Emannuel, *The Long Twentieth Century*, Verso, 1994.
Bartlett, Robert, *The Making of Europe*, Penguin, 1993.
Brewer, Ben, *Marxist Theories of Imperialism*, Rontledge and Kegan Paul, 1980.
Browne, Harry, *Joseph Chamberlain: Radical and Imperialist*, Longman, 1974.
Cain, P.J., and Hopkins, A.G., *British Imperialism: Innovation and Expansion 1688–1914*, Longman, 1993.
Cannadine, David, 'The Empire Strikes Back', *Past & Present* 147, May 1995.
Chamberlain, M.E., *The Scramble for Africa*, Longman, 1974.
Cottrell, P.L., *British Overseas Investment in the Nineteenth Century*, Macmillan, 1975.
Davis, L.E., and Robert Huttenback, *Mammon and the Pursuit of Empire: The Political Economy of British Imperialism 1860–1912*, Cambridge University Press, 1986.
Edwards, E.W., *British Diplomacy and France in China 1895–1914*, Clarendon, 1987.
Eldridge, C.C., *Victorian Imperialism*, Hodder & Stoughton, 1978.
Fischer, Fritz, *Germany's Aims in the First World War*, Chatto and Windus, 1967.
Flint, John E., *Sir George Goldie and the Making of Nigeria*, Oxford University Press, 1960.
Galbraith, J.S., *Crown and Charter: The Early Years of the British South Africa Company*, University of California Press, 1974.
Galbraith, J.S., *Mackinnon and East Africa 1878–1895*, Cambridge University Press, 1972.
Gallagher, John and Ronald Robinson, 'The Imperialism of Free Trade', *Economic History Review* 6, 1953.
Gann L.H., and Peter Duigan, *The Rulers of British Africa 1870–1914*, Croom Helm, 1978.
Hall, A.R., *The Export of Capital from Great Britain 1870–1914*, Methuen, 1968.
Harcourt, Freda, 'Disraeli's Imperialism, 1866–1868: A Question of Timing', *Historical Journal* 23, 1980.
Hechter, Michael, *Internal Colonialism*, Routledge and Kegan Paul, 1975.
Hobsbawm, E.J., *The Age of Capital 1848–1875*, Weidenfeld & Nicolson, 1975.
Hobsbawm, E.J., *The Age of Empire 1875–1914*, Weidenfeld & Nicolson, 1987.
Hobson, J.A., *Imperialism, a Study*, 1902, Allen & Unwin, 1961 reprint.
Hyam, Ronald, *Britain's Imperial Century 1815–1914: A Study of Empire and Expansion*, Batsford, 1976.
Hynes, W.G., *The Economics of Empire: Britain, Africa and the New Imperialism 1870–1895*, Longman, 1979.
Kemp, Tom, *Theories of Imperialism*, Dennis Dobson, 1967.
Kemp, Tom, *Industrialisation in Nineteenth-century Europe*, Longman, 1969.
Kennedy, Paul, 'Debate. The Costs and Benefits of British Imperialism 1846–1914', *Past & Present* 125, 1989.
Kiernan, V.G., *The Lords of Human Kind*, Weidenfeld & Nicolson, 1969.
Kiernan, V.G., *Marxism and Imperialism*, Edward Arnold, 1974.

Lenin, V.I., *Imperialism: The Highest Stage of Capitalism*, 1916 (*Collected Works*, vol. 22, Lawrence & Wishart, 1964).

MacKenzie, J.M., *Propaganda and Empire: The Manipulation of British Public Opinion 1880–1960*, Manchester University Press, 1984.

MacKenzie, J.M., *The Partition of Africa*, Methuen, 1983.

McLean, David, *Britain and her Buffer State: The Collapse of the Persian Empire 1890–1914*, Royal Historical Society, 1979.

Mangan, J.A., *Making Imperial Mentalities: Socialisation and British Imperialism*, Manchester University Press, 1990.

Mathias, Peter, *The First Industrial Nation*, Methuen, 1969.

Munro, J. Forbes, *Britain in Tropical Africa 1880–1960*, Macmillan, 1984.

Porter, A.N., *An Atlas of British Overseas Expansion*, Routledge, 1991.

Porter, Andrew, *European Imperialism 1870–1914*, Macmillan, 1994.

Porter, Bernard, *Critics of Empire: British Radical Attitudes to Colonialism in Africa 1895–1914*, Macmillan, 1968.

O'Brien, P.K., 'The Costs and Benefits of British Imperialism 1846–1914', *Past & Present* 120, 1988.

Olivier, Ronald, and G.N. Sanderson (eds), *The Cambridge History of Africa*, vol. 6, c.*1870–1905*, Cambridge University Press, 1985.

Owen, R., and Sutcliffe, B., *Studies in the Theory of Imperialism*, Longman, 1972.

Richards, Jeffrey (ed.), *Imperialism and Juvenile Literature*, Manchester University Press, 1989.

Robinson, R. and J. Gallagher, *Africa and the Victorians*, Macmillan, 1961.

Said, Edward, *Orientalism*, Routledge and Kegan Paul, 1978.

Searle, G.R., *The Quest for National Efficiency: A Study in British Pollitics and Political Thought, 1899–1914*, Blackwell, 1971.

Semmel, Bernard, *Imperialism and Social Reform: English Social-Imperial Thought 1895–1914*, Allen & Unwin, 1960.

Stockwell, A.J. (ed.), *Cambridge Illustrated History of the British Empire*, Cambridge University Press, 1996.

Webster, R.A., *Industrial Imperialism in Italy 1908–1915*, University of California Press, 1975.

Weiner, Martin J., *English Culture and the Decline of the Industrial Spirit 1850–1980*, Penguin, 1985.

Appendix I – Maps

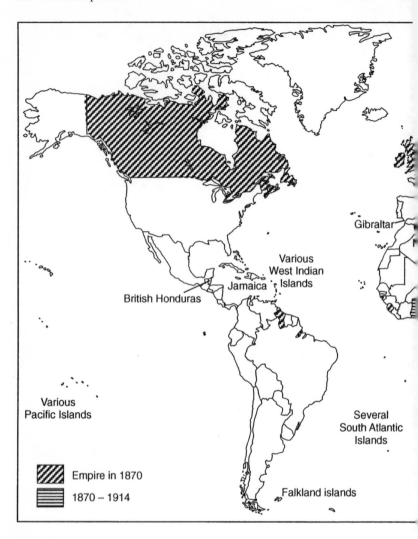

Figure 1. The British Empire 1870–1914

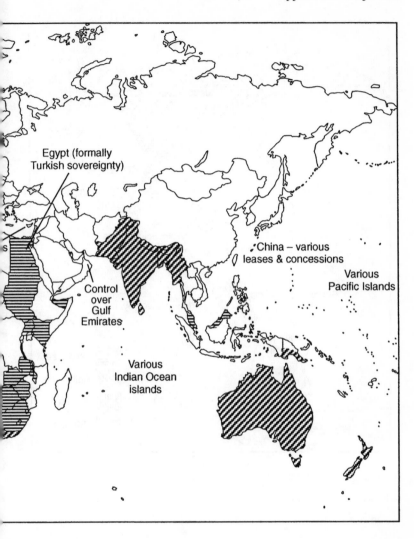

Egypt (formally Turkish sovereignty)

Control over Gulf Emirates

Various Indian Ocean islands

China – various leases & concessions

Various Pacific Islands

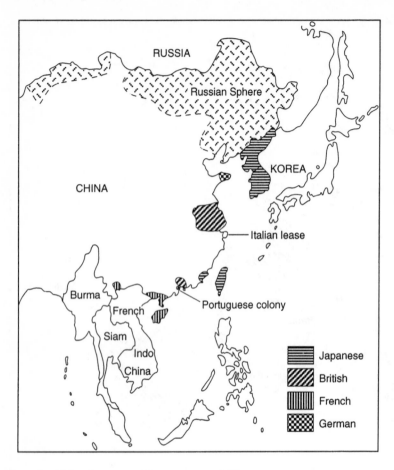

Figure 2. China: Leases and Concessions, c.1900

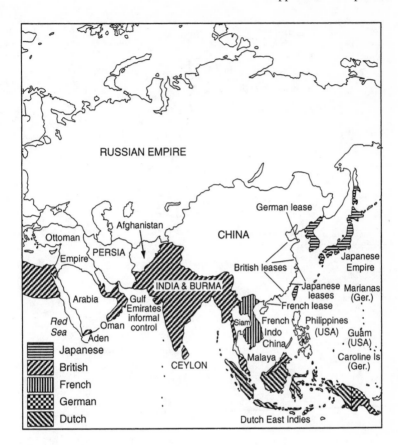

Figure 3.   Imperialism in Asia, c.1905

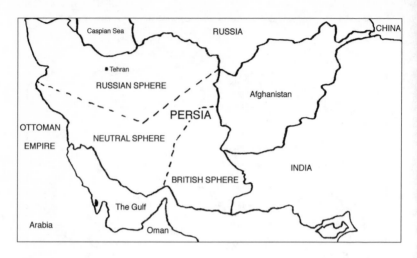

Figure 4. Persia Partitioned, 1907

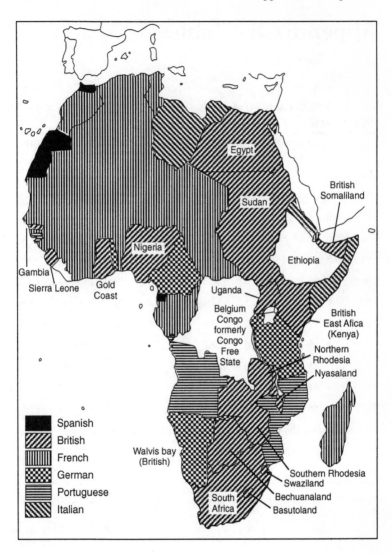

Figure 5.   Africa Partitioned, 1914

Appendix II – Tables

Table 1: Values of British trade with selected colonies and semi-colonies at 5-year intervals (£m)

	Africa (excl. N. Africa)		Asia		British N. America		India		Australia		Argentina	
	Imp	Exp	Imp	Exp	Imp	Exp	Imp	Exp	Imp	Exp	Imp	Exp
1870	6.8	4.5	42.9	34.5	8.5	6.8	25.1	19.3	11.9	8.4	1.5	2.3
1875	8.6	7.4	56.0	41.0	10.2	9.0	30.1	24.2	17.1	15.6	1.4	2.4
1880	9.5	9.4	55.5	48.4	13.4	7.7	30.1	30.5	20.4	14.0	0.9	2.5
1885	7.3	6.7	53.1	46.0	10.3	7.2	31.9	29.3	18.1	21.2	1.9	4.7
1890	9.4	13.1	56.1	53.5	12.4	7.2	32.7	33.6	21.0	19.7	4.1	8.4
1895	9.0	14.7	43.5	42.3	13.4	5.5	26.4	24.8	25.0	14.2	9.1	5.4
1900	8.4	19.7	47.0	55.7	22.2	8.1	27.4	30.1	23.8	21.6	3.1	7.1
1905	11.3	25.3	56.5	78.8	26.2	12.3	36.1	43.0	27.0	17.0	25.0	13.0
1910	19.7	34.4	79.5	82.2	26.2	20.6	42.8	48.0	38.6	27.7	29.0	19.1
1913	22.9	38.6	92.6	125.7	31.5	24.7	48.4	70.3	38.1	34.5	42.5	22.6

By comparison, the respective figures for trade with the USA were:

1870 Imports 49.8, Exports 28.3

1914 Imports 141.7, Exports 29.3

Source: B.R. Mitchell and Phyllis Deane, *Abstract of British Historical Statistics*, Cambridge University Press, 1971.

Table 2:   New British investment in selected regions at 5-year intervals (£m)

	S. America	Africa	Asia	Australasia	Total British Empire
1870	4.1	2.2	7.1	2.5	9.9
1875	8.4	4.5	4.0	6.9	18.6
1880	3.1	2.7	3.2	11.7	18.7
1885	7.1	4.7	11.0	14.9 (1886 19.4)	35.1
1890	23.3 (1889 40.2)	4.6	10.8	12.8	28.6
1895	4.1	14.9	10.4	18.7	33.4
1900	6.9	7.2	11.9	6.9	25.7
1905	13.3	29.9	35.6	3.3	54.3
1910	39.6	16.3	32.9	6.9	81.3
1913	36.2	8.1	17.4	18.8	82.9

Note: The total British overseas investment in 1914 is estimated to have been approximately £4,082,000,000 and the yearly dividend £200,000,000.

Source: A.R. Hall, *The Export of Capital from Britain 1870–1914*, Methuen, 1968.

Table 3:   British overseas investment 1865–1914 (%)

Destination			
North America	34	Independent (incl. semi-colonies)	59
South America	17	Empire	40
Asia	14	Foreign dependencies	1
Europe	13		
Australasia	11		
Africa	11		
Borrowers			
Private	55		
Governments	35		
Mixed	10		
Uses			
Infrastructure	69		
Extraction/Agriculture	12		
Manufacturing	4		
Other	15		

Sourse: A.R. Hall, *The Export of Capital from Britain 1870–1914*, Methuen, 1968.

Table 4:   Imperial Military Forces 1903 (round figures)

North America	34,000
Australia	21,000
New Zealand	15,000
Africa	42,000
India and Burma	410,000
UK	853,000
Others	17,000
Total	**1,392,000**

Source: C.S. Goldman (ed.), *The Empire and the Century*, John Murray, 1905.

Index